FIGHT FOR YOUR LIFE

AMIR KHAN

FIGHT FOR YOUR LIFE

CENTURY

1 3 5 7 9 10 8 6 4 2

Century
20 Vauxhall Bridge Road
London SW1V 2SA

Century is part of the Penguin Random House group of companies
whose addresses can be found at global.penguinrandomhouse.com.

Penguin
Random House
UK

First published by Century in 2023

www.penguin.co.uk

A CIP catalogue record for this book is available from the British Library.

Hardback ISBN 9781529907681
Trade paperback ISBN 9781529907698

Typeset in 15/19.25pt Perpetua Std by Jouve (UK), Milton Keynes
Printed and bound in Great Britain by Clays Ltd, Elcograf S.p.A.

The authorised representative in the EEA is Penguin Random House Ireland,
Morrison Chambers, 32 Nassau Street, Dublin D02 YH68

www.greenpenguin.co.uk

MIX
Paper | Supporting
responsible forestry
FSC
www.fsc.org   FSC® C018179

Penguin Random House is committed to a
sustainable future for our business, our readers
and our planet. This book is made from Forest
Stewardship Council® certified paper.

For Faryal, Lamaisah, Alayna and
Zaviyar – you are my life.

INTRODUCTION

I know this is it — the last few rolls of the dice. The last few swings of the fists. The last few desperate attempts to fend off the inevitable. And then — bang! — a blow that takes every last ounce of air from my lungs.

I'm doubled over, leaning on the ropes. There is cheering. Or is it jeering? I can't tell which — it sounds like my head's underwater. I'm gasping for air. Drowning.

I force open my eyes and remember, through the bright lights and the blurs, that I'm in Madison Square Garden. Perhaps the most iconic venue in boxing. They've all fought here — Ali, Frazier, Tyson. It's always been my dream to fight in this grand New York arena. And yet here I am, living a nightmare.

I've just been hit by a low blow from Terence Crawford. It feels like I've taken a cannonball in the shorts. The rules state I have five minutes to recover. I'll be pissing blood for days.

Boxing is a blood sport. Collapsed on that rope, I recall seeing the red stains on the canvas at my first gym and wondering what they were. My mind also turns to the first time I made an opponent bleed, and how my coach told me 'Well done!' — I liked that.

The referee comes over, checking me out. 'What do

you want to do?' I can't think straight. But I know I don't quit. I never quit. Every step of the way, in and out of the ring, I've had to fight. Even for my Olympic medal I had to battle for my right to be on that Athens stage.

What I do know is the pain is torturous. I stand, I lean, I stretch – and I double up. Nothing makes any difference. Pain is part of our sport. I fought most of my career with a broken hand. That hurts. Getting knocked out hurts too. I've done it to other fighters and they've done it to me. Haven't you heard? I've got a glass chin. That's what everyone says about me isn't it? *I've not done bad to get to Madison Square Garden with a glass chin!* I think – and then nearly throw up from the pain.

I think about the pile-on that will happen if I don't carry on. I've seen it throughout my career. Win and you're everyone's friend; lose and you're on your own. There's another version of that – win and you're British; lose and you're Pakistani. The first time I was left on the canvas, in my 'home' arena in Manchester, I've never felt more alone. Those who I thought were my friends left me at the speed of a missile.

Thankfully, my career has been one of more highs than lows. I've fulfilled pretty much my every ambition. Along the way, I've taken risks that changed me from a naive lad from Bolton to a sporting champion known the world over.

The biggest risk of all was leaving England for America. But it worked. I built a career on my own terms and said goodbye to being thought of, by some at least, as second best. It's what, ultimately, has brought me here to this 20,000-seat auditorium. I am beginning to think, though, that going back into the ring with Crawford is a risk too far.

Truth is I'm way behind on points. Miracles do happen – look at my marriage! Who'd have thought that would have survived – at times me and Faryal have definitely reached number nine of a ten count – and we're still here. But Crawford is a different proposition. This isn't a fall-out, a public spat, a storyline for a reality TV show. He's got me. If I go back in that ring, there's only one result.

The crowd is getting restless now. They can see that something's happening here – something that could bring an early end to their entertainment. The final scene of this drama was meant to be me lying flat on the canvas, three teeth in the front row, not feeling faint from a punch in the bollocks.

As a self-professed entertainer, I understand their frustration. My entire career has been built on being a crowd-pleaser. I hated the thought of being a boring boxer. I attacked, it made me vulnerable, and people loved the unpredictability. I fought in front of huge TV audiences and earned millions. And then one day I looked at my bank account and it was all gone. Which brings my head spinning back to exactly why I'm here.

Really, I should bite the bullet, go back in that ring, and take my punishment. It's all part of the game. The vulnerable card either lands face up or it doesn't, and on this occasion it most definitely hasn't. On the other hand, we're not like other sportspeople. We don't spend the hours after our 'game' in a sponsor's suite. A lot of the time we spend it in hospital. For me, tonight will be no different. And as the seconds tick by I realise I'll be happy with that. Boxing is littered with stories of those who flailed on and took one punch too many. Forget hospital – some of them never woke up at all. In that moment I think of my children. To them I'm not a boxer, I'm Daddy.

I'll be honest, I've never really grown up myself. That's got me in scrapes all my life. It's meant an awful lot of fun and an equally large amount of bad decisions. Now I'm about to make a decision that I think actually qualifies as mature. I look at Virgil Hunter, my coach. It's bedlam all around. People leaning over the ropes, cameras in my face, a dozen different voices. Even through that veil of madness I get the feeling he's thinking the same as me. Crawford's low punch has given me a way out. We both know I could fight on. We also know that to do so would be pointless. This is no longer a two-sided battle. I'm taking a beating and it's only going to get worse. There will be no lucky punch on my part, no miracle summoning of strength.

It's then that Virgil makes the decision for me – he throws in the towel. It's a sight no boxer wants to see. But at that moment I wish he was calling time on my entire career. Instead, to secure my family's future, I will have to pull myself together, forget the negative voices, ignore my crumbling joints, and carry on this crazy dance.

I'll take one hope with me from Madison Square Garden – that it's up to me when the music ends.

• • •

I want to take you on a journey in this book. But it's a journey like none you'll have been on before. How could it be? There's never been someone like me before. And actually, as I write this, I can think of one or two people who'll be thinking *Thank God!*

Some people are born to be sports stars. I wasn't one of them. I was born to be . . . actually what was I born to be? Probably, like most Asian kids growing up in the late nineties, a doctor, or a teacher. At a push I might have been a cricketer. A boxer? Come off it! No Asian lad did that sort of thing.

As it turned out, encountering boxing was the moment

I felt the rush of blood in my veins. In a single step through a dingy gym door I found my direction in life and, with some incredible guides, it led me breathless to the Olympic podium. You can overdo the 'I'm just a kid from [insert town]' routine but when you're seventeen with a silver medal round your neck it's a bit like you've swapped normality for life in a film. At that point you think you'll cruise through the next few years to the classic Hollywood happy ending.

But of course a good film needs dramatic tension. I'd never met my scriptwriter at that point so didn't realise just how much there was going to be! By the end of this book you'll have travelled more peaks and troughs than the hills that overlook my home town of Bolton.

And that's how I want it to be. I never wanted to be a boring boxer and I didn't want to write just another book. I've always worn my heart on my sleeve and, as painful as it might be, I've never held back from revealing my truth. Believe me, over the following pages I'll take you through all the amazing highs, and equally devastating lows, in and out of the ring. And by all I mean all. Including the hideous frozen-in-time moment when I heard I'd inadvertently tested positive for a banned drug – a chill I'm still trying to shake off. I don't duck anything in life, and I'll address the controversy fully in these pages.

It's only recently I've come to realise I was a champion

before I was a champion. By winning an Olympic medal as a teenager I was known by millions as something special when really I was just a kid. The days of world titles were years off, but I was seen as a big shot, never allowed to fail.

My Pakistani heritage also very quickly became a defining part of how I was viewed and I soon discovered that, when it comes to race and religion, people are fickle. As someone who had worked hard to promote unity at a difficult time for Britain, that was a massive blow, and one which in many ways led me to pursue a fighter's life in America.

That really was my 'Hollywood' dream – to be up there with boxing's greats, to fight in New York and Las Vegas. And I'm glad to say I did have those moments where I felt like a star of the silver screen. But then the reel would snap and I'd have to start building my story all over again.

The boxing has only ever been part of the story. Whether it be death threats from Al-Qaeda, gunpoint robbery, family fall-outs, marriage to a New York socialite, three kids, a sex tape, a reality TV show, a money-pit wedding hall, or walking through a flood and earthquake devastated Pakistan, I'm struggling to think of a quiet day. That means a lot of lessons learned the hard way – and you'll notice that I try to pass a few on here. I've become a teacher after all!

If a fighter makes it to the end of the battle he'll have survived twelve rounds and so that's how I've presented my story. As in any fight, some rounds you want to go on for ever; others you can't wait to get back to the refuge of your corner. I think it will be pretty obvious which are which.

Now the final bell has rung on my boxing career I'm left to move on to new and different challenges. Hanging up my gloves has given me the opportunity to reflect not just on my career but on who I am and the kind of person I want to be. Whoever that is, I just hope they get a few less slaps to the face!

I'm more than twice the age of that naive seventeen-year-old who went to Athens an unknown and came back to crowds chanting my name. I know what I'd say to him if I bumped into him now.

'Amir, you're in for one hell of a ride. But just remember, the road doesn't have to be bumpy *all* the time. It might do you good to rock back on your heels and take a deep breath once in a while.'

Now, it's your turn to take a deep breath.

Seconds out . . .

ROUND ONE

My dad knew what he was doing. He could see straight away that boxing was the answer.

As a child I was hyperactive and naughty. I had too much energy and needed a way to burn it off. I mean, how many kids do you know who were kicked out of nursery for fighting?

School wasn't much better. I misbehaved so badly that my family would literally have to go in and watch over me. I'd look up from my exercise book and there'd be Grandma staring right at me, making sure I was knuckling down. Same in the dinner hall. I'd just be thinking of lobbing a chip at a mate when I'd see her out the corner of my eye. Her face said everything – 'Don't you dare!' But they couldn't watch me all the time. The fights, and the bloody noses – usually other people's – continued. My mum once described me as 'a bit rougher than other boys'. I think she was being kind.

To be fair, a few of these fights would be in self-defence. I was short and tubby and kids from the years above would sometimes try to bully me. I knew it would only get worse if I let it happen and so if there was a group of lads giving me grief I'd target the oldest one and teach them a lesson. That had a double effect – it scared the

9

other kids off and also made the fight more interesting! It wasn't something I set out to do, but I was always the hardest kid in school. Not in a bad way – I never picked on anyone – but if people wanted to take me on I was quite happy to show them what a bad mistake they'd made. I've still actually got a mark on my hand from where I laid one lad out. I get that I shouldn't have done it but he threw the first punch. When someone was coming at me I was bound to react.

No two ways about it, I had a fearless streak, maybe because I'd had two near-death experiences before I was out of short trousers. At two weeks old I was felled by a serious chest infection which left me, by all accounts, in a hospital incubator wrapped up in tin foil like a chicken about to spend two hours on gas mark 4. I survived that only to be run over by a car when I was five. I'm not saying I sat in my hospital bed and made a conscious decision to live life to the full before illness or accident did its worst, but maybe my brain did switch to seeing things in a different way. Down the years I've often felt like pointing out to people who think boxing is dangerous that real life isn't much easier.

My family might also have to take some of the blame for the fact I was so full-on. Those early scrapes with death meant I was a bit indulged. There was discipline but I think quite a lot was let go. Looking back, rules weren't particularly something I bothered with. They usually made things quite boring – and I wasn't big on boring! That's probably why, again aged five, I climbed on top of our house. I was quite happy up there. Only when Mum threatened to tell my dad did I come down. You didn't mess with Dad.

I was a bit of a pain in the arse really. One time I took and ate a slice of cake from a teacher's desk. It looked good and I couldn't resist it. She wasn't massively impressed and once again my parents were left to do the apologising. I was reminded of this incident two decades later when, infamously, I pissed off the whole camp on *I'm a Celebrity . . . Get Me Out of Here!* by eating a bowl of strawberries and cream meant to be shared between us all. Unfortunately, Mum and Dad weren't in the jungle – this time the sorrys were down to me! There was no chance of them doubting the teacher's story. Whatever was happening every day at school was happening every minute at home too.

To be fair I did have a fair few cousins who themselves were no strangers to a bit of old-fashioned messing about. I suppose I could fling a bit of blame in their direction for the way I was, but truth is I never needed much leading astray. Fighting especially was just in me.

Dad could see exactly the kind of kid I was and knew I needed to blow off steam, get rid of some of that crazy energy. Cricket was one option. My cousin Saj Mahmood was so good he'd go on to play for England. Like him, I tried to be a fast bowler. I wanted to be firing the ball past people's ears. I did actually play for Astley Bridge in Bolton for a season, and for school too, but in the end cricket was just too slow for me. All that fielding, and then waiting ages to bat only to be out for a golden duck.

Boxing, my dad realised, would really keep me busy, push me, make me work all the time – proper tire me out! A battler himself, he also recognised my competitive spirit. He knew if I wanted to be good I'd have to really commit to the gloves. While Mum and Gran were opposed to the idea, thinking I was basically going to get beaten up, Dad got his way and so it was him who took me, aged eight, round the corner to the Halliwell Boxing Club.

• • •

I walked through the door and straight into what felt like another world. The gym was in the basement of an old factory. The smell of the place – blood, sweat, damp – hit me like an invisible right-hander. And I loved it. I'd have washed in that smell if I could. Nowadays, boxing gyms are a lot more advanced but back then a lot were like that – people shadow-boxing in front of big mirrors steamed up with condensation, chains hanging from ceilings rattling and clanking, someone grunting while pounding a heavy leather punchbag, someone else smashing gloved fists into pads held in front of them by a coach. And every now and then the DING! DING! DING! of the bell signalling the start or end of a sparring session. I looked at the canvas of the ring – *is that blood?* I was blown away by the whole experience: how fast it was, so much happening at once. *Wow! Just wow!* Right from that first moment I had only one thought – *This is what I want to do.*

I entered the gym a complete novice. Boxing was never on the telly in our house. Again, maybe that was a good thing – it meant I didn't carry any preconceptions, good or bad, in there with me. I was a young lad massively excited by what I saw and that was all there was to it. Dad was the same. He had no connection to boxing or the gym. He just knew it would give me discipline. He also liked keeping himself busy, and taking me down there and watching me progress gave him a lot back. He was going through his own learning period, eventually becoming a 'second', a cornerman, for my fights, which in turn gave him the opportunity to travel and meet new people.

I expect Dad clocked it from the off, but I was too young, too taken in by the whole crazy atmosphere to notice I was the only Asian kid there. As someone who'd never thought twice about race, mine or anyone else's, it was weeks before being 'different' from everyone else ever really occurred to me. Not that it was in any way a big deal. I'm sure I stood out like a sore thumb, but no one ever made anything of it.

After a few weeks, a couple of my friends started coming along, probably so I'd shut up banging on about it all the time. They had a go but didn't hang around long once they realised how hard it was, both mentally and physically. And so I just carried on by myself. Those twice-a-week sessions were all I thought about. One finishing was just the countdown to the next one starting, the time in between spent thinking of nothing else. Fair to say that, from the minute I went to Halliwell, boxing dominated my life. Like any kid, I'd got into all sorts of different hobbies only to get sick of them over time. With boxing that never happened. Soon I was buying my own stuff, pride of place going to a pair of pristine white gloves. I put them on and took them off endlessly.

The trainer at Halliwell was called Tommy Battle — well it was a boxing gym. It was him who gave me the basics. Like any kid, my first idea of boxing was just standing there swinging my arms. I was a veteran of more than a few playground fights and it was a style that had served me well. Tommy taught me that if I tried that in the ring I wouldn't last ten seconds. He showed me the importance of movement and footwork. One time he let me get in the ring. It felt enormous, much bigger than on TV, but I felt at home. It was a year until he allowed me to spar with another lad in there. That led to another first – real dripping blood. The lad's, not mine. I thought I'd better apologise to Tommy for going over the top but I never got the words out – 'Well done!' he told me. It had never happened like that in the playground!

Every day became a new challenge. My biggest opponent was me. I was fighting myself all the time. *Can I do it? Can I not do it?* Right there was my incentive to keep training, to keep putting the hours in. I always wanted to learn. Always wanted to be better. Part of that was understanding my character. Every time I went to the gym, I found out more about myself, the type of person I am. For instance, after I found Tommy's gym, I never wanted to fight outside the ring again. Boxing taught me self-discipline. I walked into that gym the first time a hyperactive kid who didn't know what to do with himself – someone destined to get in big trouble. I walked out somebody else completely. I was still that hyperactive kid but now I was on a different, a good, path.

While that path would eventually take me to Las Vegas and New York, the first port of call was Stoke-on-Trent. The venue for my first amateur fight was a back room in a pub, a place that had definitely seen better days. I got changed upstairs and then, accompanied by my dad and my uncles Taz and Terry, came down to a room full of cigarette smoke and bald white blokes. Nowadays you'd probably describe it as a Phil Mitchell convention. Remember, back then, not only were there no Asian fighters, but there were no Asian coaches, judges or referees. Wherever we went we were always a first. Behind that crowd, somewhere in the haze, was the boxing ring.

I recently saw the footage from that fight. Another thing that was unusual about 'Team Khan' was that we had this huge video camera, like Russian army surplus, that my uncle Taz would carry around. I'm quite glad of the smoke now, it hides the little chubby kid that I was. (For years my nickname at home was 'Fatty'! I know – subtle.) I might not have been the fittest, but I still won. Aged eleven, tactics weren't really a thing. Well, they might have been for my dad and my coach, but they weren't for me. I used to fly out of my corner and try to destroy my opponent as fast as I could. There were only three ninety-second rounds. I wanted to get on with it!

Not long after I'd started out, someone at a fight told me I'd be world champion one day. That's a big thing to say to someone who's still got their entire youth – years when practically anything can happen – ahead of them.

At the time I just smiled and lapped up the praise, but I wonder now if even then they could see that single-minded determination in me.

Very early on I lost three fights in a row. That's disheartening – easily enough to knock a young lad's confidence to the point of giving up – but I still stuck at it, and that's where I think I was different. It wasn't in me to give up. It never ever happened. That's the crux of the matter. If you want to reach the top, whatever happens, you have to stick at it. I've seen kids who look like they have world champion potential, but will they keep at it? I mean really keep at it?

Maybe I was lucky that those three defeats happened early on, when boxing was more like a hobby. But I'm also proud of the fact that, when I had absolutely nothing to lose by chucking it in, that thought, never for even one second, crossed my mind. I was too busy dreaming of being as good as Muhammad Ali, whose videos, particularly the 'Rumble in the Jungle' with George Foreman, I would watch again and again. His face was also on my bedroom wall. Every night I'd read the quote on the poster – 'I'm so fast that last night I turned off the light switch in my hotel room and was in bed before the room was dark' – and see if I could repeat the trick!

. . .

Dad could clearly see my potential and after a while took me down to Bury Amateur Boxing Club, run by a great coach called Mick Jelley. This was Mick's first gym. His modern set-up is real state-of-the-art stuff – floor mats, heating, showers – but back then we're talking holes in the roof and buckets on the floor. Toilets? 'Go outside!' Heating? 'You've got to be joking!' It was freezing cold. The only way to get anywhere near warm was to train hard. I'd look at people and there'd be steam coming off their bodies.

The electrics weren't great either. One day the lights went out. Mick was old school. There was nothing he didn't know – or thought he didn't know – about DIY. 'I know how to fix this,' he declared. At which point he grabbed a can of WD40 and sprayed it all over the fuse box. The lights came back on. Mick was delighted – 'All part of the magic!' And then BOOM! The whole box went up.

Mick always knew exactly what to say to motivate me. He told me early on that if I lost some weight he would make me a champion. I listened and not only worked hard in the gym but exercised relentlessly at home as well. In my bedroom I was doing push-ups, sit-ups, and a hundred other routines. Combined with what was basically an overnight growth spurt, I became proper physically powerful, able to hit harder and harder. I really began to show my potential, and Mick again got in my ear about how good I was looking, about how I could be something big in the sport.

But – there was always a but – I wouldn't get anywhere near the top unless I grafted and grafted and then grafted some more. Mick was right then and he's still right now. Talent is one thing. Turning that talent into real meaningful and lasting success is entirely another. There's a lot of talented boxers out there left wondering 'what if?'. I never wanted to be one of them. Give your all at anything in life and the one thing you'll never have is regrets. Mick gave me the belief that, if I truly applied myself, glory really could come my way.

Compared to the professional scene, boxing as an amateur is almost unrecognisable. Often I was fighting twice a month, not twice a year. That sounds a lot but I loved it – I'd have fought every day if I could – and it was exactly what I needed. With every fight, the ring was becoming more and more my home, my natural surroundings, my place of work.

I'd string long unbeaten runs together, not easy when you consider the amount of mismatches at this level. It wasn't uncommon to turn up to a fight and find a kid twice your size or a couple of years older prowling round the opposite corner. But I never let that intimidate me. I wanted to pass every test put in front of me, and beating kids older and bigger than me was something else that really started to get people sitting up and taking notice of this new kid on the block.

The ring had very quickly become a place I associated with winning. My confidence climbing over the ropes was always sky high, but I was never complacent with it. All the time I was learning. Some of that was transferring the technique I'd been practising in training to the fight itself. But it was more than that. No two fights are ever the same, and I was learning to adapt. As a young boxer it's so easy to get carried away when that bell goes. Adrenaline is great but you can lose your head if you're not careful, something that an experienced opponent will leap on and punish you for. I was always strong in the punch – I needed to be strong in the head too, work a fighter out, see the value of tactics.

It was an inevitable progression from club fights to regional and national championships, my first real big chance to shine coming when I fought for an Amateur Boxing Association (ABA) schoolboy title. I'd worked hard to get there, taken on some big lads in club fights, and this was my reward. I'd also beaten my opponent, a Londoner, Bobby Ward, not long before. Ward was tough, no pushover, but I trained extra hard and backed myself to do the job. On the night, though, we were hard to split and the decision went his way.

That, believe it or not, was the last time I actually cried. In the time since, I've got married, had children, and lost loved ones – but never have I cried. That's how desperate I was to be crowned under-13 champion of England. Ambition is what separates the good from the great. I wanted to make it as a boxer more than I wanted anything on earth. A year later I was back – and I made that under-13 title mine.

People started really noticing me when I began hoovering up national championships. Not only was I winning but I was taking the prizes for best boxer in the tournament. The shelves at home were groaning under the weight of all the cups and medals. My ability was shining bright, and there was no way the media could ignore it. I'd be in *The Bolton News* all the time and was being mentioned in all the big boxing magazines. Like any kid that age I'd collect all the clippings. They're probably still there in a scrapbook under a bed somewhere.

With success came something else to get used to – bigger crowds. As word of this young kid laying waste to all before him got round, I became one of the hottest amateur tickets in town, and not only to watch. Half that audience were parents of other kids desperate to see what they could pick up and pass on to their own champion-in-waiting – hopefully not someone I'd meet a bit further down the line!

By now the ABA were beginning to see they might have something special on their hands – someone who could make a mark on the international stage. They weren't wrong. I'd made what should have been a big step look easy. Taking a leap to the next level didn't faze me, just as it wouldn't throughout my career. I welcomed a challenge. I knew from the start that if I didn't put myself in the line of fire then I would never progress. I was one of many lads finding a way in the sport. Stand still and I'd soon be overtaken.

Of course, I wasn't only the best youngster, I was the only Asian youngster. 'Asian boxer' rather than 'English boxer' was the description that followed me round. That didn't particularly bother me – I was just getting on with it – but there was the odd occasion when it felt like people wanted to make it an issue. At a fight in Preston, for instance, I was beating a big favourite from a rival club when some lads in the crowd started to get nasty, one of them actually getting right up alongside the ring giving me all kinds of abuse. I don't know if he was angry that I was beating this lad or if there was something uglier – racial – about it, but soon there was spitting too. I felt it land on my legs and was so shocked and disgusted that for a few seconds I actually refused to carry on. Boxing is a sport that polices itself and that sort of behaviour is never tolerated. Afterwards, my opponent and his club couldn't apologise fast enough, although never for one minute did I blame them. There's always the odd idiot, people who'll find any reason to kick off. Thankfully, most people won't have a piece of that sort of crap.

By the time I won the ABA national junior title in May 2003 I felt pretty much unbeatable. I had become totally single-minded. Boxing was what was going to bring me fame and fortune and I wasn't going to let that chance slip away. I'd watch previews of fights coming up on Sky Box Office (we never paid for the actual fight!) and wonder if one day that might be me too – a professional boxer fighting on the biggest stages in the world. Any opponent who thought they could take that goal from me was going to get battered. I was taking massive strides in record time. I was a proper fighter on proper bills and never ever expected to come out on the losing side. That wasn't arrogance, it was knowing I had worked harder than anyone to make the best of myself. I'd overwhelm opponents with speed and power. No one could match me.

Looking back, I can see the sacrifice I made for that dream – I missed pretty much all my youth. Maybe that's why I'm such a big kid now! Once you get into your teenage years, there's a lot of distractions – girls, parties, hanging out with friends. A lot of kids quit sport between fourteen and sixteen for just those reasons. But I never did any of that.

My life was a constant round of training and fights. Boxing dominated everything. Forget hanging around on street corners, my after-school routine was get in, get changed, go for a run, get changed again, go to the mosque, go back home, get changed, and then off to the gym. Then, while my friends were heading out for the night, I'd be in bed because I'd have to be up at some stupid time in the morning for training. That takes discipline, and I can't help thinking it's beyond most people to be that single-minded at that age – to push all those diversions to one side. Don't get me wrong, it was hard. It hurt me that my friends were allowed out and I wasn't. Even if it was a night when I wasn't training in the morning, I'd have Mick calling me at home to make sure that I was in bed early so I could be up early for a run.

But while I could see I was missing out on a lot of fun and games I also knew I was seeing things most people of my age could only dream about. While some of my friends had barely been beyond Bolton, I was travelling to fights all over the place. Seeing that other side of life changed me as a person. Being separated from that usual thing of hanging around with mates gave me a broader vision of the world and the people in it.

Think about it – a lot of my boxing mates were English, be it from the boxing club or going on training camps. That culture shift was also happening in reverse. For instance, I made no bones about praying in front of the other lads. Eventually, they were pointing out it was prayer time! 'Why don't you pray, mate, and we'll catch up with you after?' If I prayed in the same room, they'd make sure they were quiet. If there was a choice of meat that wasn't kosher and a single portion of fish, they'd make sure they left the fish for me. Knowing the peace and direction Islam gave me meant they respected my religion, whereas otherwise they would probably have never encountered it. They taught me a lot and I taught them a lot in return.

I grew up fast. I'm not saying I was 'Mr Sensible' – I don't think I've ever been called that! – but it did mean I had an old head on young shoulders when it came to self-discipline, ambition and sport. I didn't realise at the time but that was a massive factor in finding success so early. When the time came to showcase myself on the bigger stages I was ready.

I'd get a glimpse of that bigger stage by going to see fights in Manchester. Sometimes I'd bump into the big-name pros I worshipped. At an England v Russia fight at Old Trafford, Ricky Hatton was watching. I asked him to autograph my programme only for him to make a big deal of getting my signature, talking me up as the next big thing. I never forgot the way he treated me that night – making me feel ten foot tall – and it's something I've always tried to do myself when meeting kids starting out. Crazily, of course, Ricky would later become a great friend – I'd have thought you were mad if you'd told me that at the time.

Naseem Hamed was another hero on my radar. The 'Prince' was a great fighter but he was also insanely flamboyant. I mean, how many boxers do a front somersault into the ring? His fighting style was so exciting, always on the attack, looking for the knockout. I thought he was an amazing boxer but I was more struck by his incredible ability to entertain. From the minute I saw him I knew he was exactly the type of boxer I wanted to be. I actually wrote to him as part of a school project, hoping day after day that I'd get a letter, signed photo, anything, back. Eventually, gutted, I gave up. Maybe that was a sign of things to come. Sadly, my relationship with Naseem always tended to be more down than up.

• • •

While I lived and breathed boxing, I'd be lying if I said there wasn't the odd occasion when my passion slipped a little. If that happened, Dad would be down on me like a ton of bricks, something to be avoided at all costs. It wasn't so much the fear of getting in trouble with him that kept me focused, it was the respect I had for him. I didn't want to upset him or Mum. If they told me to do something I would listen and do it. I also knew they practised what they preached. Dad was a mechanic with his own garage, while Mum managed everything at home, including four kids. To this day I have never seen two people work so hard.

I know for sure my fighting spirit comes from them. Like many Pakistanis, their families had arrived in England in the sixties and worked hard to build a solid foundation for themselves. Dad's family came from Matore, a village near Islamabad, a place where nothing came easy and everything had to be earned, and that attitude was instilled in me from a young age. As a kid, I'd be taken there to visit relatives and see a bit of family history. I'll be honest, it didn't mean that much to me at the time. Having grown up in Bolton, where everything I could ever want was right on my doorstep, going to Matore really did feel like being chucked into the middle of nowhere. Very quickly I'd be restless and bored. 'OK, we've seen the village – what now?' That other-worldly feel was made worse by the electricity going on and off all the time. Where was Mick Jelley when you needed him!

But for my parents and grandparents, Matore was a big deal. They were seeing the village from completely the other way round. This for them had been normality, a place of friendship and camaraderie. When first my grandad Lall, followed by his wife Iqbal and their children, left Matore, England had been the other-worldly place. My dad was nine when he arrived in England. Imagine that. One day he was in a quiet little village in Pakistan, sun beaming down, the next he was in a grey northern industrial town on the edge of Manchester. As a child you never see the world through your elders' eyes. But I totally get it now. I see what a big sacrifice my grandparents made for a life they hoped would bring more opportunity for them, but, more importantly, their children.

Eventually, my parents invested in a house in Islamabad and we would stay there instead. We were delighted – no more Matore! Again we were thinking only of ourselves. The city was where the shops and malls were. Before, when the big announcement came – 'We're going to Pakistan!' – we'd bite our tongues. Inside we'd be thinking *Oh no! Matore!* When the house in the city happened, suddenly it was smiles all round. Kids eh? I just hope mine never groan inside when I tell them we're leaving Dubai, where they live most of the time, to spend a few weeks back in Bolton!

I might be the dad now, a few decades on from that naughty little kid who once drove his own parents round the bend, but I've never forgotten what my dad did for me by introducing me to boxing. I still get the same kick out of walking into a gym, especially Mick's. While the set-up might be smarter, there's one thing that never changes – the personalities.

In a boxing gym you always end up bumping into some crazy characters, full of energy – mouths and fists running away with themselves. Thankfully I like being round people like that. Why? Because I see so much of myself in them, in particular the lad taking a bashing in a sparring session because he's got carried away and forgotten all the basics. At that point, Mick's voice always comes back to me. 'Keep it simple, Amir!' – it's like I've been transported back a quarter of a century. I'll talk to the kid. 'Keep your hands up,' I'll tell him. 'Just move around. Don't overthink what you're doing. Do more than you need and you'll end up getting caught more.'

Simplicity was the best lesson any coach ever taught me. The young boxers who try too hard and do everything at once are the ones whose talent goes to waste. Want to be a boxer? Take it slowly. Take a deep breath and chill.

Mick showed me that being a successful boxer was as much in the head as the fists. Meeting him was the moment that supercharged my life. Over the years I saw him more and more as not only a great trainer but a true and lasting friend. Actually, I'd go further – Mick became another father figure, a man whose advice I never stopped appreciating wherever I was in my career and whichever big-name coach I was with at the time. I paid my respects by making sure he had a ringside ticket for my fights all over the world and paying for his hotel and flights. It was the least I could do – without him, none of it would ever have happened. I'm sure some people thought it was a bit odd for me to like having my old amateur coach around – it's definitely not the done thing in professional boxing – but the way I saw it he knew me better than anyone. His job as a trainer might have been to bring through future generations, but this generation of boxer always wanted to hear his advice.

Why? Because, for all the big moments that were down the track, without Mick I'd have never experienced what I still consider the best of them all . . .

COACHING SESSION I

Whatever it is you want to achieve, in sport or life in general, there's one thing you need more than anything else – the very best people around you. They might fall into your lap or they might need a bit of searching for. Either way, without them the journey will be twice as long and hard.

There isn't a boxer out there who made it without a ring of trusted advisers. They are the people who know exactly how to motivate you, how your mind and body works.

That's why, when I see kids training at my own gym, I'm fine with telling them how well they're doing but I'll always add, 'If you want to make it, you'll have to keep training really, really hard', because it's that graft that will act like a beacon to the best coaches and trainers. They'll give everything for you – but only if you give everything back.

Never stop working, surround yourself with the right team, and you're well on the way to being the best.

ROUND TWO

My rise through the sport was meteoric — well, that's the word I saw a lot in the papers at the time. I wasn't just being talked of as the best in my age group in England but potentially the world. For me, there was only one place to test that out — the World Cadet Championships, the biggest youth competition out there. I'd already won the European Cadet Championships and European Schoolboys Championships, taking the best boxer accolade at both, and the global stage was the next step.

The ABA agreed — at least about the global part. Trouble was they wanted me to take a different path — to the Junior Olympics in Detroit. For me, compared to the Cadets, the Junior Olympics was secondary. The Cadets had to be the best route forward. But the ABA thought differently and so off to the US I went, little knowing that, as with my later career, a trip across the Atlantic would be a big step on the road to glory.

Victor Ortiz was the number one kid in America and would later go on to be welterweight world champion. In the final I stopped him in the second round. I overwhelmed him with quick clean punches and a full-on attacking style. The Americans were stunned, especially since I'd already beaten their number two to get to the final. They

could see something me and my team hadn't considered –
replicate those performances at the Olympics proper in
Athens in a year's time and there was a decent chance of
a medal. None of us had ever thought for a minute that
competing at the Games in 2004 was a possibility. Beijing
in 2008 maybe, but I'd only be seventeen when Athens
came around. You have to be eighteen to box at the
Olympics, don't you? After all, that was how old you had
to be to be categorised as 'senior' by the ABA. Wrong,
said the Americans, you can fight as a senior at the
Olympics aged seventeen. The Americans seized on that
confusion immediately. 'If you can't fight for Britain, why
don't you fight for us?'

It was a shock. What, now I'm suddenly American?
How does that work? My only real association with
America was watching *Baywatch* on TV. 'Not a problem,'
our hosts assured me. The green card would be ready and
waiting.

Fighting for America was never really an option for
me. I was British, had always fought under the Union
Jack, and didn't want that to change. Anyway, if I could
go to Athens aged seventeen, what was to stop me doing
so with my own country?

The answer to that was the ABA. The powers-that-be
had decided the Olympics was no place for boys to come
face to face with men. So dismissive was their reaction

that we actually thought the Americans must have got their facts wrong. We listened and headed back to Bolton thinking that was that. But I couldn't help wondering why the Americans would be flashing the promise of green cards around if there was nothing in it. They wouldn't do that without knowing the facts. The internet came to my rescue. I had a look at the Olympic rules and there it was – seventeen – in black and white. I wasn't going to have my dream trampled on, and neither was my dad. I was entitled to go. Obviously I'd have to go through all the selection criteria, but no one should be blocking my path.

Looking back, getting to the Olympics was a harder battle than pretty much anything I faced when I got there. To be on that plane to Athens I'd have to convince the ABA that I had what it takes not only to qualify but to stand up to the test of facing adult boxers. That process began with again winning the European Cadets. Actually, I didn't just win it, I blew away my opponents and won best boxer. I had outgrown that level. Nothing, though, seemed to change. When the subject of me going to the Olympics was raised with the ABA you could hardly hear for the sound of air being sucked through teeth.

I can thank England coach Terry Edwards for finally breaking the deadlock. Terry was more of the school that 'if you're good enough, you're old enough'. I was offered a hoop to jump through. For me, the European Schoolboys Championships in Italy effectively became a preliminary Olympic knockout round. I smashed it. *OK*, I thought, *surely that's it*. But while Terry fought my corner it felt like we were up against a tag team of ABA officials. The door was slammed shut again. I was massively disappointed. It felt like I'd done everything I could to show I was ready for the next level and that taking on adult fighters wasn't a problem. But they weren't going to listen. Nothing was going to change their minds. They knew best and that was that.

With time running out it felt like we'd reached the end of the road. And then we had an idea. Fear of missing out – or FOMO – is something that's talked about a lot these days. Not so much in 2004. Maybe we were forerunners! We told the ABA that if they didn't let us box in Athens for Britain we'd box for Pakistan. While claiming US heritage might have been stretching it a bit, competing under the flag of Pakistan posed no such issues. My parents and grandparents were born there and I'd been there myself on several occasions. We hoped the ABA would panic that they were about to see potential Olympic glory disappear to a rival country. I'm not saying I was nailed on for a medal – far from it – but there was always a possibility. The ABA could have been left with egg on their faces if that happened.

The plan worked. Finally, they saw the light. But it had been a risk. Had I aligned myself with Pakistan that would have been the end of it. I'd have walked out at the opening ceremony under their flag. Don't get me wrong, I love Pakistan, but I'm British through and through.

I was quickly dispatched to a training camp in Sheffield. The next hurdle in the journey would be to prove I could do what I'd so confidently claimed – take on sparring partners with age, experience and, maybe, strength on their side. The kinds of people who were unlikely to take massively kindly to a seventeen-year-old who seemed to have the sun permanently shining out of his arse.

I think because I looked so young, coaches thought I was naive. I wasn't. I'd been watching adults boxing for years. I knew that a lot of the basic elements – strength of punches, technique, stamina, intimidation – would be different. They weren't going to collapse under the first punch. They would stand their ground and hit back. I also knew I could match that by being a very good boxer, not just physically but mentally. One thing having a lot of amateur fights – and a few at nursery! – teaches you is to read an opponent quickly. Think about it – in a three-round fight, with an unpredictable and unknown kid in the opposite corner, you can't afford to waste too much time sussing them out. Everything happens so fast, like it's being played out at triple speed. It turned out, as we'd argued all along, that I was totally capable of getting in the ring with adults. I'd passed the first test on the way to Athens. There were plenty more to come.

Sparring is one thing. The ABA wanted to see me fight. I was sent to a tournament in Germany and, after years of pretty much cruising past opponents, it was probably the shock to the system I needed. My first opponent was a proper tough guy, Germany's number one lightweight, at his peak in his mid-twenties. At one point he really caught me and I was given a standing count as I tried desperately to stop my legs from buckling.

Not only getting through that fight but finding the strength and resilience to recover and win it was a massive learning curve for me – especially since the final round came as a total surprise. Slumped in my corner, looking forward to a welcome rest, Terry, who'd travelled out with the British lads, looked a bit confused. 'You do know these fights are four rounds not three?' Getting up and going again was a huge mental and physical test. I didn't enjoy it, but if I was to get to the top in the sport these were the internal battles I needed to win.

I went on to win the tournament and, with (another) best boxer prize in the bag, the ABA now knew I was the real deal. Seventeen or not, it didn't matter. I had shown I could compete as a senior. Now, instead of stalling, they started to back me. They selected me for the Olympic qualifiers ahead of their own reigning ABA champion.

. . .

I'm not sure people realise this, but the Olympic qualifiers are in some ways a bigger test than the Games themselves. Split into regional groups, a bit like the World Cup in football, the European section has always been tricky, but it had been made much harder after the Soviet Union split into fifteen different nations. Whereas before you'd have a handful of boxers competing under the banner of the USSR, now there were dozens of tough, tough fighters in the mix. If anything was going to make me look like a kid it was these guys. They all looked like they'd had fifteen years in the army. I looked like I worked in a sweet shop.

The size factor was a bit intimidating, but one thing I never lacked was confidence. My track record told me I had nothing to fear. I didn't expect anyone to be a pushover but I was convinced I was the best fighter there. Then disaster. My first fight was against a Georgian guy. He was a good few years older and the look on his face said he thought he could eat me for breakfast – and then boil the bones up for dinner. In fact I more than held my own and, when the bell rang for the final time, I felt I'd won quite comfortably. The judges, though, called it the other way. I couldn't believe what I was hearing. It was a horrible feeling. I'd battled so hard to get to this stage, had worked so hard to persuade the selectors I was the best option, and now this.

There was no time to sit and wallow. There was another qualifier in Bulgaria coming up. There is only one response to losing – do all you can to make sure it doesn't happen again. We pored over the video of the fight and tried to cement up whatever cracks the Georgian had exposed. And that's why when, crazily, mine and the Georgian's names were paired together again, what might have been a moment of panic was actually one of relief. It was a chance not only to repair the damage of the defeat but emphasise how much I was the better fighter. I did both convincingly.

All the way through that tournament, my slight build, my youth, worked to my advantage. My next opponent looked at me like something you'd put through a sausage grinder. He was like a dog let off a leash and when the bell rang went straight for the jugular. That might seem intimidating, but actually a boxer who does that has lost control. They are fighting on assumptions. His was that his greater age and physicality meant he could simply trample me into the dirt. Instead he ran straight into the perfect left hook. He fought on but it was like he was on half power. The dog was struggling and the referee put him out of his misery in round three.

That left just two fights between me and Athens. The whole thing was starting to feel unreal. It seemed like no time since I'd started boxing and now an Olympic place was a real possibility. I could quite easily have got over-excited but somehow kept my feet on the ground.

The next fight was with the experienced Romanian Adrian Alexandru, as solid as they come. Me, Terry and Mick analysed video after video trying to find a weakness. But he was robotic in his brilliance. In fact, at one point Mick's only solution was 'hit him as hard as you can' – which to be fair does work a lot in boxing!

Eventually, we saw what had been obvious all the time. The best way to face a robot is to interrupt their rhythm. I'd try not to let him settle. Trouble is the best boxers are guaranteed to have done their homework too. The Romanian, who was roughly twice my age, was not going to let some kid waltz into the ring and boss him around. He'd got a good idea of how I'd try to stop him and barely gave me an inch to do so. But when those inches came I took full advantage. I hit him – hard (good old Mick!) – and managed to get ahead of him on points. Now if I could just hang on . . .

With the seconds ticking down, everything was on

me. By now I was the only English fighter left with a chance of making it to Greece. The anxiety in the Great Britain camp was obvious. To have no fighters at the Olympics would raise a lot of questions, be an embarrassment, and potentially affect future funding. Not that any of that was going through my mind. All I was thinking of was getting through the non-stop trading of punches. It was a level of exhaustion I'd never experienced. At that point only adrenaline is getting you through.

Finally, the bell rang. I was through to the final. Except there would be no final. My opponent pulled out and that was that. Athens here I come! I was so happy to have made it, but I'll be honest, half of me was just as happy to have proved all those doubters in the ABA wrong. Remember, if they'd had their way I'd have been spending the summer of 2004 watching the Olympics on TV.

As it turned out, my battles with the ABA weren't over. I desperately wanted to fight in the World Junior Championships in South Korea a few weeks before Athens. It was a big ambition of mine and would, I thought, offer a handy warm-up for the action in Greece. The ABA thought differently. They insisted it was an unnecessary injury risk before the Olympics. Ironic really. They'd started out before the Olympics arguing that the seniors were too risky, and now I was at the Olympics the juniors were the ones posing a threat.

The resulting stand-off was familiar. We kept arguing our case. They kept saying no. I didn't want to miss out on a last crack at being crowned world junior lightweight champion, a massive achievement for a young boxer, and so eventually said I'd forfeit my Olympic place and fight in South Korea instead. It was a bit like the Pakistan situation all over again, except this time if I had to make a choice I really did want to go down this other path. Sounds mad to think I'd put anything above the Olympics but up to that point I'd fought as a junior all my life and really wanted to prove I was best in the world. I had only a few months left as a junior. I had my whole life as a senior. Again it put the powers-that-be in a really difficult position. Could they really afford to see their only Olympic hope walk away? The answer was no. They backed down. I could do both. Great. What could possibly go wrong?

The biggest argument the ABA had for me not going to South Korea was the risk of injury, by which they meant a hand. As a seventeen-year-old, that sort of talk is nonsense. You're unbreakable. Injuries are something that affect old people. And then barely had I stepped in the ring over there when I caught my right thumb really clumsily on the head of a Cuban. The pain was excruciating and immediate. I carried on and still won but my hand was swollen to the size of a grapefruit. If it was confirmed as a break, that would be it.

I'd gone to South Korea thinking I could compete in both tournaments. Now it looked like I'd get nowhere in either. For a while it was touch and go but the physio was confident there was no fracture. It would hurt – a lot – but I could carry on. I did exactly that. 'I know I can do this!' I thought. I pretty much won that tournament with one hand tied behind my back. For the last three fights I could hardly use my right, although I still laid one lad flat out with it. If the judges had ever sussed I was fighting with an injury I'd have been slung straight out. I certainly wasn't going to tell them and made sure it didn't stop me lifting the trophy.

The Olympics were now only a month away. For a while the hand injury was a worry but by the time I got on the flight to Athens it was pretty much gone. Not that it mattered. Again, I'd have fought with one hand if I'd had to.

At this stage, things were still pretty low-key. There was interest in Bolton about a local kid fighting in Athens but that was about it. I wasn't on the national radar. The big hopes for Great Britain were in the athletics stadium, velodrome and swimming pool. Believe me, when the Games kicked off on 13 August no one was shouting about

Amir Khan in the boxing – well, except everyone in our house!

• • •

Any thoughts of trying to keep the Games low-key in my own head, treating them like just another tournament, were blown away when I arrived in the Olympic Village. I was used to travelling to competitions by now but the Olympics was different scale. I'd watched the previous Games in Sydney on TV and never really given much thought to how it all works behind the scenes. When you're actually in it, it's mind-blowing.

The Olympic Village is one of the most bizarre places on earth. You're wandering around, going to get something to eat, or coming back from training, and there'll be a megastar walking the other way. Maybe for people used to multi-sports tournaments this is normal, but I had to literally stop myself pointing at people, jaw on the floor, and saying their name out loud. Kelly Holmes! Denise Lewis! Matthew Pinsent! These people were everywhere. It was actually quite humbling to be in their company. Any other time I'd have maybe asked for an autograph but that seems a bit weird when you're on the same team!

My only disappointment was that, again, there'd been

a little bit of friction with the ABA. Terry, as the national coach, was always going to be in my corner in Greece but I'd always hoped Mick would be there too. They'd both been a massive factor in getting me to this stage and together offered me fantastic encouragement and advice. As a club coach, though, Mick couldn't get accreditation from the ABA. Not that there was anything to stop him coming out anyway. He might not be there in my corner but he was still able to meet up with me elsewhere and tell me his thoughts on how I should play it in the ring. For me that was massive. An Olympics is a big step up for any athlete – I didn't realise it at the time but I was Britain's youngest Olympic boxer since welterweight Colin Jones in 1976 – and Mick, who'd known me so long, was the bridge between Amir the kid and Amir the Olympian.

In the lightweight division there was one name that every competitor wanted to avoid – Mario Kindelán. The Cuban was the most fearsome pound-for-pound amateur in the world, virtually unbeatable, and in his absolute prime as three-time world champion and reigning Olympic gold medallist. If Cuban sportspeople had been allowed to compete professionally, he'd have definitely been a champion in that world too.

I'd already encountered Kindelán in a pre-Olympic tournament, the Acropolis Cup, a sort of scene-setter where fighters could get used to how things would be in Athens. I was on a bus back from a training session when another lad looked up at me. He'd just seen the draw – 'You've got Kindelán in the first round.' I think I was meant to look disappointed, maybe a bit scared even. Instead all I felt was excitement. A nervous excitement but still excitement. I was going into the ring with the best amateur in the world. What's not to like?

The coaches were more wary. Again, there'd been division as to whether I should even travel to the Acropolis Cup. Some thought that as an unknown quantity there was a risk of me giving my game away to rivals. I never saw it like that. As ever I just wanted to get in the ring and face the challenge. If anything, coming up against Kindelán was a bonus. If we did meet in Athens I'd have had a good look at him. There's no point running away from the best. If you're any good you'll have to fight them some time.

The fight itself was, quite literally, man versus boy – at the time I was often referred to in the media as 'The Kid'! Kindelán was twice my age, ten times more wily, and a hundred times more experienced. He beat me but I held my own, and actually felt the fight was closer than the score of 33–13 suggested. I came back to Bolton with a definite thought in my head – *he can be beaten*. Although I knew that to test that theory out in Athens would mean me reaching the final. Kindelán's place in it was all but guaranteed.

By the time the boxing got underway towards the end of the Olympics, the Great Britain team had won loads of medals. It felt like I was really part of something, and I was even beginning to get used to day-to-day life in the village. Any feelings of 'normality', though, were blown away when I drew the local hero Marios Kaperonis in the first round. From a smoky back room in a pub in Stoke I'd now spun through time to a baying crowd in a 13,000-seat arena in Athens. I don't care who you are, how mentally strong, that's going to be a massive shock to the system. Terry did his best to calm me, to make me remember I was fighting Kaperonis not the occasion, but I'd not yet encountered anything like this. It felt a bit like I was watching myself from the outside rather than being in the actual moment, and the Greek lad, with the crowd behind him actually started to inch ahead. If I hadn't realised what was going wrong, and made myself relax, that could have been the end of it there and then. As it was, I stopped him in the third round.

As with Audley Harrison, who'd taken gold in the super-heavyweight division in Sydney, the British media could see the shoots of a story developing. I was used to a couple of newspaper blokes and the odd TV crew; now in the post-fight press conference it was standing room only.

I was too caught up in competing to realise it but the tale of a seventeen-year-old Asian lad from Bolton taking on the world was starting to capture an audience back in the UK. All of a sudden people were beginning to know my name. They were interested in me. They wanted to see how far I could go.

Two days later, I was back in the ring, this time against the European champion, Dimitar Shtilianov. It's a fight I don't remember too much about, other than most people expected him to beat me. This time, though, I was on my game from the off. I breezed past him, sending the hype into overdrive. Win my next fight and I was in the medals. Everyone wanted a slice of me, I'm hoping because they thought I could win, not because I was all there was left to talk about now pretty much everyone else in the British team had gone home.

The South Korean Baik Jong-sub was next in the quarter-final. I stopped him in ninety-seven seconds. He hit the floor. I picked up a bronze medal.

In beating Baik I became the youngest boxer to win an Olympic medal since Floyd Patterson at the 1952 Helsinki Games. Floyd went on to be heavyweight champion of the world. Everyone was going mad, and this was when I really began to understand how big this whole thing was getting back home. Not just a few mentions on the sports pages, I was now front-page news. I actually got to see copies of the *Daily Mirror* and *The Sun*. There was my face staring back at me. I was a student at college and I was getting the kind of coverage usually given to footballers and A-list celebs.

Thankfully, I didn't let it go to my head. Terry would remind me I was here to do a job, but he didn't need to. The coverage was great, and I'd be lying if I said I didn't like it, but it didn't detract for one minute from what I was trying to achieve. Before anything, I was a sportsman, determined and competitive. Every fight I ever went into I'd do everything I could to win. No matter where I was in my life, what the distractions, I never let anything get in the way of my goal, and the immediate target was to turn bronze into silver or gold.

No one knows that desire better than other sportspeople, and over the next few hours I took calls from Lennox Lewis and Audley Harrison bigging me up, plus I received a letter from Ricky Hatton. Getting my autograph really had been a good call! I especially appreciated Audley making the effort. He knew exactly what it was like to be in my position. Not that I needed much down-to-earth advice. In fact, when a reporter asked about my state of mind, Terry replied: 'It's him who has to calm me down!'

After Baik, everyone thought I'd do the same to the Kazakh, Serik Yeleuov, in the semis. I would never be that arrogant about any fight, but even so I was surprised at just how hard he came at me. I was losing after the first round and even when I pulled myself together and started landing some punches it made little difference to an electronic scoring system that seemed to be marking a different fight. It would have been easy to have let irritation turn to panic. Instead I boxed clever and made sure I caught him as many times as possible. By the end of the fourth round I was miles ahead.

I was an Olympic silver medallist, with a shout at getting the gold. And there was me thinking nine GCSEs wasn't bad! Millions had watched me do it and millions more would tune in for the final. Somehow I'd become not just the amateur boxing story of the year, but the boxing story of the year full-stop. Back in Bolton my friends were going mad, as was half the country. It felt like anyone I'd ever known was being asked for information and quotes about me. I was being compared to the great names of the past, like Sugar Ray Leonard, who'd won gold for the USA aged just twenty. I wasn't a great student of the sport but I'd heard his name mentioned often enough to know it meant something. I was getting love from everywhere, even Mario Kindelán. At the weigh-in he congratulated me and gave me a hug. Imagine that at a pro fight! As a pro the weigh-in is a time to intimidate and call each other names. He'd do the same if he saw me around the village. I had massive respect for him as both a person and a fighter.

. . .

For me, Kindelán was almost a free hit. I had everything to gain and absolutely nothing to lose. That meant nerves wouldn't be a big deal. In fact, all the way through the Olympics the pressure never came from the fights; it came from myself so desperately wanting to prove that this was where I belonged. That was my own competitive nature, but it was also a hangover from the battle I'd had with the ABA just to be here.

I had no fear of Kindelán. I wasn't going into that final with the mindset that I was going to lose. I looked back to that pre-Olympics fight and knew I could push him much closer to the line. What had got me to this stage was lightness on my feet, hand speed and sheer power. I would need all that and more against Kindelán. He was a master of points-based tournament boxing. Relying on the counter-attack, he invited his opponent to come on to him and then cashed in. His defence meant he could build a lead and then easily hold on to it. His opponent would have to take risks, and taking risks against Kindelán has only one outcome. My challenge was again to disrupt my opponent's rhythm, to slow down a little, not get sucked into going punch for punch. If I could match Kindelán's point-scoring, even maybe inch ahead, he would have to rethink. Could an opponent whose tactics had worked so well for so long adapt like that? We hoped not!

The fight, at the Peristeri Hall, in the heat and dust of an Athens summer, did have a bit of a gladiatorial feel to it – the young kid versus the gnarled and unbeatable champion. I was half expecting Russell Crowe to appear. He didn't – but, incredibly, another Hollywood star did. Perhaps the greatest underdog of them all. As I sat in my dressing room preparing for the fight, there was a knock on the door. I looked up and there was Rocky. I know! Rocky! As in Balboa! As in Sylvester Stallone! I thought I was dreaming. Maybe this whole thing was a dream! He had popped in to wish me well. 'You can do it, man! You can do it!' Unbelievable. Maybe he had a bit of sympathy. After all, no one gave Rocky a cat in hell's chance either. For a kid who had watched Rocky battle through those epic fights it was totally surreal.

The fight came right at the end of the Games. As well as my mum, dad, brother and sisters, a fair few of my fellow Great Britain team-mates, such as the sprint relay team, were in the audience too. That was without the thousands of British fans who'd managed to get tickets. Walking into the arena I could hear my name being chanted. Unreal. As a seventeen-year-old I didn't have many hairs on the back of my neck but the ones I did have definitely stood up.

After a cagey first round, I was actually 4–3 up. The second was where I lost it – 11–5 in favour of a fighter like Kindelán was always going to be a tall order to overcome. The third round went his way 8–5 but I matched him 8–8 in the fourth. By then, though, I'd left myself far too much to do.

I was disappointed not sad. I hadn't disgraced myself. I had no regrets. I'd lost 33–13 to Kindelán in the Acropolis Cup. Within a few months, I'd narrowed that to 30–22. Against the best amateur fighter in any division in the world, a bloke who was winning tournaments when I was a baby, I'd shown I could hold my own. Losing to Kindelán, an all-time great, at that stage was no disgrace. He was nothing but respectful in victory. He hugged me and told me it would be my turn next time round – he had vowed to retire after the fight. To be his final opponent wasn't a gold medal but it was an honour in itself.

I looked around the arena and was pleased to see smiles not tears from fans, family and friends. Same with the medal ceremony. I can still see the look on my sister Tabinda's face as she caught the flowers I chucked from the podium. It's weird because normally in boxing, like any sport, finishing second is a disappointment. Finishing second means you've lost. But so much of what happened after the fight felt like a celebration. I'd achieved so much, so young, that silver somehow felt like victory. Everyone, the massed ranks of media included, wanted to congratulate me, not commiserate. I'd lost but I was still the story of the Games. I knew I'd been fighting hard for years to make the grade, but to most people I'd just popped up from nowhere. I was the boy who'd taken on men and, aside from the brick wall of Kindelán, had come out on top. It was a good enough story not to need a fairy-tale ending.

With the Games done, the Great Britain team boarded the plane to London. Between us we'd won plenty of medals, building on Sydney four years previously, and we knew from the stuff we'd seen in the papers that there was a real buzz back home. Nothing, though, could have prepared us for the fan and media frenzy that awaited us at Gatwick. I thought everything would be about Kelly Holmes, who'd won two golds on the track, maybe Chris Hoy and Bradley Wiggins, who'd done the business in the velodrome, but with my name ringing round the South Terminal – 'Amir! Amir!' – it seemed that most of them were waiting for me.

The minute I stepped off the plane I got my very first autograph request. I didn't know what to do! I scribbled my name as fast as I could. Believe it or not, I've stuck with the same signature ever since. That was the first time I felt in any way famous. Pre-Olympics, I'd been in the local paper a few times, on regional TV, but this was different league. People were wanting photos signed, pointing cameras at me. I was like, *Wow! This has never happened before!* People were so excited to see me.

It didn't stop there. A couple of days later we flew up to Manchester. If anything the scenes were even madder. I needed a police escort to get through the crowds and into the Hummer limo that had been laid on for me to take me back to Bolton. No chance of an inconspicuous arrival! Not that it mattered. I could have headed home in a Nissan Micra and the welcome would have been the same. I literally couldn't get into my street. People were everywhere trying to shake my hand and take pictures. It seemed that half the town had turned out to see the local hero.

It was decided that a parade was the best way for people to congratulate me and for me to show my appreciation for Bolton's incredible love and support. Beforehand I stood on the steps of the town hall draped in the Union Jack. For once I wasn't the centre of attention. My dad had outdone me by having the flag made into a waistcoat. We all then boarded an open-top red London bus with 'Congratulations Amir!' across the front. Driving round those packed streets that just a few weeks earlier I was walking totally anonymously really was quite something. I also took my medal along to Bolton Wanderers' game with Manchester United at the Reebok Stadium. As I waited in the tunnel to go on the pitch, Ryan Giggs and Roy Keane shook my hand. There were so many of these insane 'Hang on a minute . . .' moments I could barely keep up with them.

Soon after, it was back down to London for a big medal-winners open-top bus parade in front of 200,000 fans before meeting the Queen at Buckingham Palace. I'll be honest, I didn't know you weren't meant to speak to her and wasted no time in finding out if she'd seen my fights.

'Are you going to keep on going?' she asked me. I told her that hopefully next time I'd be coming home with the gold. If a conversation with the Queen wasn't enough, I was also cornered by Prime Minister Tony Blair asking me for an autograph for his kids.

For a while it felt like that was how it was going to be for ever. I'd have trouble going into Bolton or even to the local shop without being mobbed. People had respect for me. I'd made a name for myself in a tough sport by virtue of putting in a lot of hard work. Then there were the people who kept stopping me to say: 'Do you know how much you look like Amir Khan?'! I loved seeing the looks on their faces when I told them I was the real thing.

A minority, though, weren't quite so friendly. They couldn't help showing hate and jealousy. I had it a few times – 'You think you're a fighter? Come on then, let's have it.' I'd walk away. I couldn't comprehend why anybody would get like that. Maybe they didn't like the fact their girlfriend liked me, or hated the fact I was the centre of attention. Who knows what was going on in their heads.

I'm not saying it was easy to walk away from in-your-face aggression like that, but I had to. It would be me, not them, who'd be plastered all over the papers. I'd be the one in the shit. The effect it did have was to make me realise I should never engage with negative people – a complete waste of time and energy.

Thankfully, there were far more positives than negatives. The Boxing Writers' Club, for example, voted me Britain's Best Young Boxer of the Year, the first amateur to receive the accolade in its fifty-three-year history. But bigger than that was the door into boxing my performance gave to young Asian lads. Before Athens, boxing just wasn't a thing in the Asian community. Parents didn't want their children to go into a sport like that. They wanted them to be doctors.

I'd had it myself. Because I had to leave the mosque fifteen minutes early to get to training, a teacher there would ask why it was so important for me to go to the gym. 'What's boxing going to do for you?' I remember those words so clearly. He would laugh afterwards because he really thought it was a total waste of time and effort. I think about how things might have panned out for me had I listened, had I respected – as I was meant to – what he said.

I knew that attitude was blinkered, and it looked like a lot of other kids did too. Before my success at the Olympics, Mick's gym was only open Mondays and Thursdays. Afterwards, it got so busy he opened two extra days. A lot of that was down to a big influx of Asian lads – another reason why for me the Olympics is one big happy memory.

In truth, I still consider the Olympics my best moment. It's funny, but one of the things I remember most about Athens is the announcement before every fight – 'Representing Great Britain, Amir Khan!' Those words, and then winning a medal for my country, were so special. They meant so much to me. To then see the reaction – everyone celebrating me as a British lad fighting for my country – made me feel so proud. I had no reason to think it wouldn't last.

Typically, the medal itself ended up shoved in a drawer. Looking back, that's a bit sad. When something has taken blood, sweat and tears to achieve, it shouldn't be hidden away. But sometimes it takes someone else to point that out.

Recently I got it back out and, along with the picture of me meeting the Queen, put it on display in my house. These are the things I always want to be remembered for. I want my kids to see them every day while they're growing up. I want them not only to see what their dad did, but to understand how hard you have to work to achieve success.

Nothing in life comes easy. The years after the Olympics would prove that. But no matter where I was in my career, in my life, memories of those Games, and the road to Athens, would always give me a boost.

I was seventeen years old and I did all that.

COACHING SESSION 2

I'm a big believer in 'If you don't try, you'll never know'. There were a lot of times when I could have been overwhelmed by the speed of the progress I was making, by the constant challenges, in and out of the boxing ring, that were coming my way.

At that point I was just barrelling through life. I didn't think about my actions with any depth. Now I can see that I owe every great memory to my willingness to jump right in. I should really have been a diver not a boxer!

Only in the big wide world outside your comfort zone will you find the real you. It's there that the most incredible experiences are to be had.

Make that jump and you might just be surprised where you end up.

ROUND THREE

I'd spent two weeks in Athens. I'd grown up about ten years. That was the kind of progress I was making. Everything about me was so much better. Pro fighting gets all the attention, but never underestimate the value of amateur boxing. It's where those long pro careers are built. Lessons are learned quickly – they have to be.

Inevitably, all the talk after the Olympics was about me turning professional. Frank Warren, one of the biggest promoters in the UK, was particularly vocal about the possibilities, stating publicly that I was better already than a lot of the pros out there and that it wouldn't be long before a world title was mine for the taking.

If that wasn't mad enough, Oscar De La Hoya, one of the absolute giants of world boxing, a pound-for-pound legend, made contact. Having won the Olympic lightweight title himself at just nineteen years old, the American knew the quandary I found myself in. He'd taken the decision to turn pro, and it hadn't been a bad one. He was a world champion at twenty. Oscar's plan was for me to up sticks and move to the States where I'd join his LA-based Golden Boy Promotions stable – as a fighter, 'Golden Boy' was Oscar's nickname. It was insane. I hadn't even decided whether to leave college let alone leave Britain! And now a nailed-on hero of mine was offering to take me under his wing and let me loose in America.

It was tempting beyond belief. Just put yourself in that situation. Whoever your hero is, they ring you up and say: 'Hi, mate, I think you're great. Come over and I'll make you one of the biggest stars on the planet.' Believe me, it takes a lot to say no. But at the same time I was only seventeen. The amateur scene was where I belonged. The Commonwealth Games in two years' time and potentially the Beijing Olympics in 2008 looked the better road, giving me a chance to develop physically and pick up some more titles along the way.

There was another factor – the kind of pros I'd be pitched against early in my career were unlikely to be half as big a test as the very best amateurs. In terms of progression as a fighter, learning the trade, staying in the amateur ranks made sense. While big figures were being dangled in front of me and my family by various promoters and consortiums, there was more to think about than money. Grab that cash now and my career, and earning potential, might suffer in the long run.

As the 'hero' of Athens, I was now the one to beat. I was a moving target and in my first fight back, a regional round of the ABA Championships at Preston Guildhall, my opponent hit the bullseye and put me flat on my arse.

It was no more than I deserved. I'd been playing to the crowd a bit and was holding my hands low. That's what you get for showboating.

I got up and came back to win convincingly but afterwards I noticed that elements of the media really went to town on the story. I was a bit shocked. I'd heard it said a few times, 'They only build you up to knock you down', but had never really thought it to be true. I suppose that incident was the start of an up and down relationship with the press that would continue for many years. There would be times when they went for the kill more than any opponent.

I was as desperate to do well in the ABA Championships as people were to see me. My fights always attracted sell-out crowds and to make sure my supporters didn't miss out the ABA always made sure we had a few hundred tickets. But when it came to the quarter-final tie at Great Yarmouth suddenly there was only a handful coming our way. I was upset. I knew the problems that poor ticketing could cause. As a junior I'd seen it first-hand at a venue in London when half the fighters' families and friends couldn't get in and all hell broke loose.

My team could see the same happening at Great Yarmouth and went back to the ABA to ask for more tickets. They weren't moving. Out of their hands, they said. I could see the headlines, the potential for trouble, even if they couldn't. I wanted that title, the biggest in amateur boxing, but not if it meant people being hurt. We said we'd pull out if it wasn't sorted and we meant it. Eventually, way too late in the day, 300 tickets miraculously appeared. Forget it, we told them. If it could be sorted now, it could have been sorted days earlier. So I pulled out.

It was just the latest example of the ABA causing unnecessary friction. Any other organisation would have made an Olympic silver medallist their poster boy. I was the best advert for boxing, for spreading its appeal across new areas of the population, they could ever have wished for. But so many times we felt like they never saw what they had in their hands. It had been like that before the Olympics and, sadly, it was exactly the same afterwards.

What really stuck in my throat was the championships finals. Unable to fight, we went down to offer our support. Before the actual boxing, the ABA was presented with more than a million pounds by UK Sport to prepare talent for the next Olympics. I sat there and wondered how much that cheque would have been for had I not won a medal in Athens. My mood wasn't helped any when I thought about the battle I'd had with the ABA to even get there. I wasn't expecting the red-carpet treatment at the finals but at the same time I didn't expect to be a doormat.

It felt like every single time I wanted something from

the ABA they put up the shutters. Same when a Great Britain versus Cuba fight was announced. Everyone could see what a chance that was for a big rematch of me against Kindelán before he finally hung up his gloves. Everyone that is but the ABA. I hadn't won the senior title – because I hadn't wanted a riot at Great Yarmouth – and so they said I couldn't fight Kindelán. The audience, for a repeat of an Olympic final watched by millions, would have been massive, yet another great advert for amateur boxing, but instead the ABA strangled everyone's dream with red tape.

Our response to that was simple – 'OK, if you won't do it, we'll do it ourselves.' We decided we'd get Kindelán on a show organised by Bury ABC. No sooner had the ABA got wind of the idea than their well-oiled obstruction machine hit gears we'd never imagined. First up they said Kindelán had amateur commitments in both Ireland and Cuba and so a date couldn't be sanctioned. Then, when finally, with Frank Warren as mediator, the ABA did agree a date, they messed up the visas needed by Kindelán's team. Only at the last minute was the situation saved, again by Frank and his people.

If the ABA wanted to push me away, to lose me from the amateur ranks, then they were going the right way about it. It hadn't gone unnoticed how Frank had worked hard for us, guided us through the minefields. For sure, his world looked a lot brighter, a lot more professional than sticking with the ABA. I, for one, was sick of the constant battles. Frank, one of the most respected names in the sport, who knew boxing inside out, was offering a carefully planned introduction to the pro world. It was agreed that immediately after the Kindelán fight I would announce I was going professional. I had just turned eighteen. Frank reckoned I could be a world champion by twenty-one.

And so Mario Kindelán, the Cuban legend, came to Bolton. He was put up in the hotel at the Reebok Stadium. From there he wouldn't have far to travel to the fight. Neither would I. It was at the arena right next door.

That night, in May 2005, is one I will never forget. Kindelán was the biggest fight I could possibly have had at that time, one that half the country wanted to see, and it was in front of thousands of my own fans in my home town. 'Amir Comes Home!' it said on the front of the programme. I didn't want to let anyone down.

Eight months had passed since Athens and I'd thought a lot about what else I could have done to beat Kindelán. I came up with a plan – this time I'd fight with my head as well as my heart. I wouldn't give him the chance to rack up the points like he had in Greece, wouldn't launch at him, but play a careful game, landing some good blows before retreating out of reach. As plans go, it worked a treat. I never put myself in danger and the result was a hard-fought, but totally deserved victory – 19–13 in my favour across four rounds.

Of course, the cynics couldn't wait to have a go. They said Kindelán was only going through the motions; that the fight meant nothing to him. They were wise not to say that to his face. You don't achieve what he did in boxing by switching off. Kindelán was a proud man. He fought to win every time. Anyway, the doubters were dwarfed by the sheer number of people who loved every minute of the occasion. That last showdown with the Cuban was watched by 6.3 million viewers on ITV, the channel's biggest Saturday night figure of the year. Again the ABA had been shown precisely what they'd be missing – and I'd been shown the future. Frank had made a deal that my fights would be shown on ITV from then on. Although none of us could ever have imagined the significance my first professional fight would take on.

· · ·

I don't suppose many people remember the fight itself. Against David Bailey, again at Bolton Arena, it lasted just 109 seconds. What they will remember is the events of nine days before. On 7 July 2005, four Islamist suicide bombers killed fifty-two people by letting off devices on three Underground trains and a bus in London. When I saw those pictures of the carnage, I was as shocked and sickened as anyone. Suddenly the focus was right on the community – young British Asians – that I was the best-known part of.

The fight had suddenly taken on a whole different meaning. I knew I had to make a statement of unification, to let people know that the actions of those four killers in no way represented the views of the rest of the Asian community. In front of several thousand fans and the live TV cameras – again the fight was being shown on ITV – I made my way to the ring to the strains of 'Land of Hope and Glory', while my younger brother Haroon carried a Union Jack with 'LONDON' emblazoned across it. To my baseball cap I'd added a black ribbon.

A few minutes later, with the fight done and dusted, I dedicated the victory to everyone caught up in and affected by the blasts. I held up that same 'LONDON' flag and carried it round the ring. 'Look,' I was saying. 'I'm Asian, I'm of Pakistani heritage, and I love Britain. I was born here.' I wanted to emphasise that was how 99.99 per cent of all Asians felt about the country. I wanted people to know that the Asian community wasn't separate. We were as sickened and disgusted as anyone by 7/7 and stood alongside everyone else at a truly horrible time. Asians in the audience carried the same message – a giant flag had been made joining the Pakistan and Great Britain colours together and the words 'No Terrorism' written on it. There weren't just my fans in the arena that night. People had travelled from all over to support other fighters on the card. As I looked round, I was massively warmed by the fact that they were cheering too. In the record books it just says that I knocked Bailey out in round one. That night was much, much more than that.

The pressure on me at that time was enormous. Here I was, a young lad just setting out on a sporting journey, and now it seemed like I was representing the whole Asian community. I was the one standing there waving the flag for all the Muslims, condemning what had happened, and appealing for unity. I was a sportsperson not a spokesperson but it was me getting up and giving my thoughts on the situation. People were looking to me as much as anyone to condemn the actions of the bombers and say out loud to others who may be being radicalised that it was the wrong way. At the same time, and this was where the flag came in, I wanted people to know that Asian people respected the UK. We respected the Queen. We respected everyone. In my case, I had enjoyed opportunity in Britain that I'd never have found anywhere else in the world. In every interview I did I made that clear – 'without this country I would not be here'. I meant it and I truly wanted to show my appreciation. None of it was ever made up. I just hoped that someone like me speaking out would help the country to heal.

While a lot of people thanked me for standing up and speaking out against hate, there were others who turned against me. At one point Al-Qaeda even made a threat against my life. I wasn't scared. I'd always spoken the truth and I wasn't about to stop now. At the end of the day, life's in God's hands. That's the way I always see these things. It was quite funny actually. I couldn't help thinking: *How are these people even going to find me in a place like Bolton?* I felt like saying: 'You're more than welcome to come and have a look!'

It's often forgotten that at the Bailey fight itself there was a bomb threat. The night ended with the arena evacuated and everyone out on the street, including the two fighters boxing after me, with police dogs everywhere keeping people back from the arena. Thankfully, it was a false alarm, but it was another kick-in-the-guts reminder of just where we were at that time.

Looking back, it still amazes me how I became a central figure in that whole awful situation. I'd seen after 9/11 how so much suspicion had been directed at the Asian community, but I'd never expected to be the one called on to smooth over tension and misunderstanding. It seemed like I was the one every journalist wanted to talk to. I was described in *The Independent* as 'a standard-bearer among the Muslim community in combating terrorism' and in another paper as 'the single most important role model for a multinational British society'. Me? A standard-bearer? A role model? I wasn't much more than a kid.

I'll be honest, it upset me after a while – 'Am I the only prominent Asian in the UK?' – but then I worried that if I said I didn't want to talk it would look bad. I was in a difficult place at that time. It wasn't just 7/7, if anything about radicalisation was mentioned I'd be the one the news channels looked to for a reaction. To them I was the face of all Asians out there. I'd get phone calls all the time – 'What do you think of this?' But at the same time there had to be someone to do it. And it looked like that person was me. I didn't have a choice.

I think part of me being the go-to voice came from not being nervous of attention. That meant from an early age I never tried to be anything I wasn't. When people asked me to speak, they knew I was going to say it how it was. Every interview I've ever done – TV, newspaper, podcast, whatever – I've stuck 100 per cent to being me. There have been times when publicists have suggested I do media training. No way. Why would I do that when people like me and listen to me as I am? You see it on TV all the time – sportspeople giving boring stock answers because they've been told to rein themselves in. Do that and you kiss goodbye to both your honesty and personality. Not only that, but every person watching that interview

can see through it. They know it's not you – that the real
you has been put in a straitjacket. On occasion, in the
run-up to a fight, or to answer an enquiry, I've been asked
to read a prepared statement. I can't do it. I'll take a pen
to it to make sure it reads like I'd say it, because then I
can be true to myself. I think it's so negative, harmful
even, to stop people being themselves.

So hectic were those few weeks after 7/7 that I found
myself desperately trying to hang on to a bit of normal
life. I didn't want to be seen as the one talking about
terrorism all the time any more than I wanted forever to
be labelled the 'lad from the Olympics'. I just wanted to
be me. People were amazingly supportive but sometimes
it could get embarrassing. I'd go out for some food with
mates and the owner would come over and say the whole
lot was on the house. That was so generous but at the
same time I didn't want anyone to think I was playing the
big 'I am'. As far as I knew, the only person I knew who
didn't have to pay for stuff was the monarch!

• • •

I was also trying to maintain my focus on boxing. It was
like I'd been sidetracked into being a politician rather
than someone setting out on a sporting career. I wanted
to throw myself 100 per cent into fighting. After the

Kindelán bout I'd actually gone out to Cuba and seen how much the sport meant over there. I loved the full-on, no holding back attitude of their fighters. Right there I'd seen the type of boxer I wanted to be. That desire would be backed up by watching Latin American fighters such as Marco Antonio Barrera and Erik Morales and, from the Philippines, the great Manny Pacquiao. They were so exciting to watch, possibly because they were so attack-minded there was always a chance, however slight, for their opponent, and wherever I ended up in the sport I wanted to be remembered as an exciting fighter, one who put bums on seats.

I was already well on the way to developing the incredible hand speed and foot movement that would become my hallmark. If that attacking style also meant I had an element of vulnerability, then so be it. To fill arenas and be wanted by TV you need to sell tickets – and nothing sells tickets more than vulnerability. People might be surprised by me being so open about my own commercial appeal but the minute you become a pro you have to be aware of your value. This isn't a hobby any more, it's your job – a job that can hit a brick wall at any time. When that last fight came I wanted to be remembered, like all the boxers I worshipped, as an entertainer, and I knew that vulnerability would make me more of a show.

It's not all sportspeople who will admit they're entertainers but I've got no problem with it at all. It's why, while I did shore up my defences a bit later under Virgil Hunter, I never stopped trying to be attacking. I could have been a boring boxer, plodding my way through fight after fight, but I didn't want to be that person. I wanted everyone to be on the edge of their seat. Even now I'll come across a clip of myself on Instagram or TikTok and be shocked by just how good a lot of my fights were, how quick my hands were, how exciting it all was. In my mid-thirties, and with a bit of distance, it's like I'm watching those clips as an outsider, like it isn't me. That's a bit weird, but it also means I can really appreciate what a great spectacle it was.

Any sportsperson who got the crowd on their feet I loved at that time. Unbelievably – I still loved my cricket – I would find myself training alongside Andrew 'Freddie' Flintoff at a gym in Salford. This was peak Fred, the same time he was brushing the Aussies aside with bat and ball in the Ashes of 2005. He'd shown his support for me by attending the Kindelán fight. That wasn't a bad night, but if I could ever have 30,000 people on their feet like Fred I'd be well happy.

Fred's history, well documented by the tabloids, suggested he'd combined his rise to the top with a love of a few beers and big nights out. That was one way I wasn't going to follow in his footsteps. For one, I didn't drink. And two, I had no intention of moving out of home. My family had been my foundation for everything I'd achieved and I had no intention of changing that now. Exciting in the ring, quiet out of it, suited me fine – for now.

. . .

With the pro debut out the way – a fight that had grabbed the national attention in a way I could have never imagined – I was looking forward to a bit more of a routine bout in my next outing, against the Coventry fighter Baz Carey. Instead, it would be an encounter that affected the entire rest of my career.

I beat Baz convincingly. The problem was that at one point I hit him on top of the head with the same hand that I'd injured on the Cuban's skull at the World Juniors a year earlier. There was a bit of pain but when I then caught him awkwardly on the point of the elbow, that pain became a really sharp jolt. It was on top of the hand in the area of the metacarpals, the bones that attach the fingers and thumb to the wrist. It was bad enough to make me wince, but you get twinges like that in boxing. They come and go. Thing was, when I punched hard with my right hand it happened again. Thankfully, it was only a four-round fight and I was well ahead on points or else it might have been an issue. The bell went thirty seconds later and that was that. I took off my glove and my right hand had mushroomed out of all recognition.

For the next thirteen years it would never be the same again. Punching with my right hand would always be uncomfortable. The obvious thing would have been to stop after Carey and have an operation, which was what a specialist advised, but I was young, just arrived on the pro scene. I didn't want people to think I was one of those guys who has two fights, gets injured and disappears. Then there was the TV contract, and the money that came with it. Take six months, a year even, out of the sport and all that would disappear, as would my pathway to the big fights I craved. That was a lot to walk away from when there was a simpler alternative – don't tell anyone. Well, at least outside of my immediate circle. As far as I was concerned, so long as I could make a fist I'd carry on. And that's exactly what I did. I got wise about looking after my right hand and took extra care to make sure my left was always solid and never at risk. Injure my left hand too and that was it, I was done for.

Sometimes I'd have a cortisone injection before a fight to numb the pain. I would have the hand bandaged into a fist – the only way I could make one – which would be agony, especially since pro gloves tend to be smaller than at the amateur level, and then in would go the needle.

Only then could I punch hard. When I found out that these injections give a short-term fix but can cause long-term ligament damage I stopped doing them. I'd just have to get used to the pain, which was exactly what I did.

Essentially, from the point when I hit Baz Carey on the elbow, my right hand was compromised by 50 per cent. It was the best-kept secret in boxing. If fighters had known that weakness was there to be exploited, I'd have been finished. As it was I got away with it for years. In fact in one of my early pro fights I actually hit someone with my right hand and cleaned him up. Again, that gave me the confidence to carry on without treatment. Looking back now, it's inevitable that I wonder what I might have achieved without carrying that injury. I don't just mean in terms of winning more fights with the extra firepower, but that all-important mental positivity as well.

Hand injury or not, it's easy, if you're not careful, to get carried away with your own publicity. As I prepared for my third pro fight, against Steve Gethin, however, something happened to remind me that the world very much did not revolve around me. News started to trickle in of a huge earthquake in northern Pakistan. It soon became clear that this was a disaster of immense magnitude. Around 75,000 people had been killed and among them were family members of friends of ours. We'd been lucky.

By the time, a month later, I was back in the ring against the Sheffield boxer Daniel Thorpe, I could see the quake slipping off the headlines. I hated the thought of it becoming yesterday's news and wondered if I could put my name to some use. By going out there maybe I could raise awareness of the continued need for aid.

In December I flew out and visited a camp for some of the three million people left homeless by the disaster. What I saw was deeply upsetting. Seeing the pictures on TV had been bad enough, to see it with my own eyes was overwhelming. Young kids had been left orphaned. Food was scarce and shelter basic. Children were stood in T-shirts in the freezing cold. I hated the thought that they had been forgotten, that the rest of the world had moved on like none of this had ever happened. I appealed for clothes, food, blankets, anything that would make life just that little bit more bearable, maybe even give a little hope. I was nineteen years old and again was seeing a side of the world far removed from my sheltered life in Bolton. I knew right from that point that being a famous boxer would be nothing if I didn't give anything back.

On a national scale I became an ambassador for the National Society for the Prevention of Cruelty to Children, again meeting the Queen at a reception at St James's Palace in London. My first step towards giving back in Bolton, meanwhile, was investing in a community gym. Future Prime Minister David Cameron gave a speech at the opening. He knew what I knew – that a place like this was massive for keeping kids off the streets and steering them to a better future. 'It is something that we can all really applaud,' he told the audience. 'He is a role model and a hero to people.' That was nice to hear, but actually I was always happy in the background. I just wanted to give other people a chance.

· · ·

I'd had a couple of reminders that I still needed to do a bit of growing up myself. I'd been convicted of careless driving and banned for six months, with a £1,000 fine, after injuring a pedestrian in Bolton town centre. I was banned again for driving at high speed on the M62. It was a wake-up call. My family weren't impressed and I knew I had to learn lessons about acting more responsibly. I knew that the gym would help to keep me grounded, remind me where I'd come from. It made me smile when a teacher told me that since a couple of lads had started there they'd been behaving themselves in school. Who did that remind me of?

I'd started earning some decent money, which meant I could take on projects like the gym. I'd added the Commonwealth lightweight title, not to be confused with the Commonwealth Games title, to my growing list of achievements and was routinely boxing before the TV cameras in some of the biggest arenas in the country.

Predictably, as I cast aside one opponent after another, there were snide comments from some quarters that my path into the professional ranks had been too smooth. Another way of looking at that was that I'd been way too good for the fighters who'd so far stood in my way. As Frank Warren was more than happy to point out to the critics, winning the Commonwealth title when still only twenty was not the act of someone who'd been taking things easy, especially since I'd had to beat Willie Limond, a tough Scottish boxer, who, with twenty-eight wins from twenty-nine fights, was as hard as they come and actually had me on the canvas before he retired with a broken nose.

It wasn't just the sportswriters who felt they needed to put me under extra scrutiny. I was beginning to see that the media in general might look to land a blow to my reputation. For the aid visit to Pakistan I did an interview with a journalist. In the subsequent feature he made a big deal of how, on a trip organised by Oxfam, I'd worn my Reebok sponsored gear rather than the Oxfam logo. It was the classic non-story – in photos I was contracted to wear Reebok stuff and that was the end of it. Oxfam hadn't been bothered, they were just glad I was helping with their appeal, and so was I. But the underlying message was clear — that I was out for myself. The same article also made ugly insinuations about the fact my family were so heavily involved in my management. Everyone in my camp was upset. What had we done to deserve this? I didn't see other young boxers and their families getting this kind of treatment. I'm no different in real life to how I am as a boxer. If I'm under attack I'll come out fighting. We took action against the newspaper and they paid damages, which went to charity.

I could at least console myself with the thought that features in the big newspapers reflected my growing stature in the sport. Defending my Commonwealth title, I went the twelve-round championship distance for the first time in beating the Guyanan, Gairy St Clair, before taking a big leap towards my ultimate goal by beating the Dane, Martin Kristjansen, at the Bolton Arena in an official eliminator for the World Boxing Organization (WBO) lightweight title. In the meantime, I took the WBO's Intercontinental belt by stopping him in seven rounds.

After the fight I thought long and hard about the next stage of my career and the kind of experienced coach who could help me make the transition to the big time. It was for that reason I split from Oliver Harrison, the Salford trainer who'd overseen all seventeen of my pro fights to that point. It was never anything personal against Oliver. I always had the biggest respect for him not just as a trainer but as a mentor. One of my favourite things was to sit and listen to his own stories of being a boxer. I loved every bit of it. As a new pro it was amazing to be around someone like Oliver. I was massively grateful for the work he'd done but any successful sportsperson will tell you that the key to progress is to keep learning. I was now in world title territory. I needed a coach who knew the challenges I would face, someone to teach me how to be that extra bit special.

I went over to Las Vegas to support Welsh super-middleweight world champion Joe Calzaghe in his 'Battle of the Planet' fight with US counterpart Bernard Hopkins. While I was there I trained briefly with the absolute legend that is Floyd Mayweather Jr. That trip to the States was big for me. Floyd, who had seen it, done it, bought the T-shirt, gave me a few words of advice – 'The best are the best in and out of the ring!' and about building and maintaining a career at the top of the sport – and I even had a session with his trainer uncle Roger Mayweather.

Back in the UK I trained for a while with Dean Powell, a great bloke who had coached former British world champions Duke McKenzie and Lloyd Honeyghan. I'd known Dean since I turned pro. He worked with Frank and had been a big voice in selecting my opponents as I rose up the ladder. Dean had one of the best boxing brains in the business. He knew exactly where I needed to improve with the fundamentals and before long he'd rejigged my footwork, giving me extra reach, and, with a series of foot-numbing runs, made me fitter than ever.

I'd need both advantages if I was to retain my Commonwealth lightweight title against Michael Gomez at Birmingham's National Indoor Arena. While the Irishman was at the fag end of his career, he wasn't going to roll over and let a kid – that's still actually how I was seen by a lot of people – like me deny him a title. As it turned out I put him on the floor twice and the fight was over in five rounds, although Gomez landed some decent blows.

Fights were getting tougher and tougher. Opponents were hitting harder and harder. Every bout was a reminder that I had entered a world where people would stop at nothing to win. As a young boxer, confidence comes from facing up to those people, showing them that you are not afraid and that, if anything, they are the ones who should be worried. That's how you progress. All the time you are building towards the next level, weaving your way through a maze of fights and fighters. The key is always to face boxers who are beatable but will add something to your reputation. For that you rely on the team around you. Get it wrong and you are in trouble. Big trouble. As I was about to find out.

COACHING SESSION 3

Whatever you want to achieve in life, chances are there will be someone standing in the way. I saw it myself on several occasions early in my career when certain people and organisations decided they knew better and tried to deny me big opportunities. I didn't listen. Some might say that's me being stubborn — actually I've always listened to advice from others. But if I know in my bones that I am being treated unfairly I will never sit back — I will always fight.

Remember, there are always ways to get round barriers. People in sport, and life, want you to jump over their hurdles. That's fine if they're fair. If they're ten feet high with barbed wire on top it can get a bit tricky.

When that happens, take a detour. There is always another path to victory.

ROUND FOUR

Flat on my back on the canvas at the MEN Arena in Manchester, I was struggling to comprehend what had happened. The bell for the start of the first round had only just gone and now all I could see was a blur of bright lights and faces staring down at me.

Actually, it had been fifty-four seconds since the bell. In that time, my opponent, a little-known Colombian by the name of Breidis Prescott, had turned me inside out and put me through a mincing machine. The result was the mess now lying on the floor. Somewhere at the side of the ring my mum was in tears. She was so upset she was actually being given oxygen.

In the end I'd gone with the Cuban, Jorge Rubio, as my new permanent trainer. Based in Miami and with a great record as coach of the Cuban amateur team, the idea was he could inject a Latino edge into my boxing. He came on the recommendation of the cruiserweight world champion David Haye, who had worked with him in the past. I liked David and so had a couple of sessions with Rubio, liked what I saw, and thought he was ideal to take me to the next level. I was particularly impressed with how he encouraged a hard, attacking style while not compromising on flair – the classic Latin American way I so loved.

The coaching side of things was great. Where Rubio tripped up was selecting Prescott as my first fight. The guy in the other corner should actually have been the American, Kevin Kelley. Until Rubio mentioned Prescott that's where we were, and that was the fight, and the style of fighter, I was preparing for. It's usually the promoter's job to matchmake, to pick the right fights, and Frank felt Kelley, as a former world champion, was the kind of big, but beatable, name who offered a good step up to the next level.

At that stage I felt I'd done enough to have a crack at a world title. Frank wasn't so sure. He had his feet firmly on the ground and was concerned about me travelling through the ranks too quickly. He felt I needed to be patient, to carry on for a while with my 'schooling', and that Kelley ticked a lot of boxes on that progression. Frank always had an eye for a good storyline. He knew that Kelley's history with Prince Naseem, who'd knocked Kelley out in Madison Square Garden, would spark interest in him heading over to fight the Prince's 'successor'.

It was then that Rubio stepped in – 'Look, I've got this guy Prescott. This is the man you need to fight. Honestly Amir, he'll be better for you. He's young, unbeaten, and a big hitter. He covers so many angles for you.'

A coach wouldn't normally do a promoter's job any more than a promoter would get the kit on and start coaching, but Rubio really did feel the Colombian offered more than the ageing Kelley. On the face of it Prescott sounded tough. He was also taller and naturally heavier, usually a light-welterweight rather than lightweight, but Rubio was adamant there'd be no problem.

'You'll beat Prescott easily and at the same time you'll be able to prove a point – that you can take a punch. After this fight no one will say "boo" to you.' Looking back, that was a bit odd. At that time I'd never really been tested. Rubio was trying to prove a point that didn't need to be proved. Whatever, we were either too naive or too respectful and so went ahead with his choice.

It was the wake-up call to end all wake-up calls. I came out of my corner too quick and Prescott wasted no time in landing some good shots, catching me with a sharp jab that immediately set me back on my heels and got the legs wobbling. It was the left hook a few seconds later that really did for me. At that point I really should have gone into full-on defensive mode and tried to kill the seconds and ride out the round but instead, and this is where inexperience comes in, I tried to counter-attack. I was in no state to do so. A classic left, right, goodnight and it was all over. On my home turf, with 99 per cent of the audience there to see me put on an exhibition, and my Sky Box Office debut, it's hard to think how it could have gone much worse. It still counts as my worst video nasty, and one which would forever haunt me. From that point on I never heard the end of the 'fact' that I had a glass chin.

Recovering the next day, I couldn't help thinking a wrecking ball had just smashed straight through my career. Worse, it was a wrecking ball that could so easily have been avoided. The more I thought about it, the more angry I was with Rubio. I'd been put in front of someone with a big punch who saw me, everyone's favourite Olympic silver medal winner, as his big chance to make a name for himself. Rubio should never have pushed that fight – and we should never have listened.

It wasn't just that. I thought about the training too. In the week before a fight what usually happens is you ease back – by that time the work is done. But with Rubio I was still doing twelve-hour sparring sessions. I was being pushed too hard. I was tired, I was unhappy, and because I was still training, and so getting bigger and stronger, I was struggling to stay at the required weight. Add into that the communication difficulties – Rubio couldn't speak English – and it really wasn't a good mix.

I was also massively underprepared in terms of my knowledge of Prescott. I'd literally only watched a couple of rounds of his. That was a definite mistake. It meant I

Beat Kell Brook in my final fight and, to my fans and to me, I'd be a champion one last time.

February 2022. I had only one thought as I walked into the auditorium before the Kell Brook fight – *I DON'T WANT TO BE HERE.*

That's not to say I went into that fight expecting to lose. While I knew I wasn't the fighter I had been, I also knew that physically and mentally I was better than Kell.

Back to the beginning where it all started: 27 August 2004 at the Peristeri Olympic Boxing Hall in Athens, Greece. After defeating Serik Yeleuov of Kazakhstan in the men's boxing 60 kg semi-final.

By winning an Olympic medal as a teenager (in Athens, 2004) I was known by millions as something special when really I was just a kid. The days of world titles were years off, but I was seen as a big shot, never allowed to fail.

My dad knew what he was doing. He could see straight away that boxing was the answer . . . Dad could see exactly the kind of kid I was and knew I needed to blow off steam, get rid of some of that crazy energy.

With Dad – Shah Khan (*left*) and my first Amateur Boxing coach, Mick Jelley (*right*).

Mick always knew exactly what to say to motivate me. He told me early on that if I lost some weight he would make me a champion. I listened and not only worked hard in the gym but exercised relentlessly at home as well.

Landing a brutal shot on my way to beating Barrera on 14 March 2009.

Daring to be great. You either do it or you don't.

Personally I never wanted to waste my best boxing years going through the motions.

May 2016. During my fight with Canelo Alvarez – I later faced a knockout from Canelo in round six.

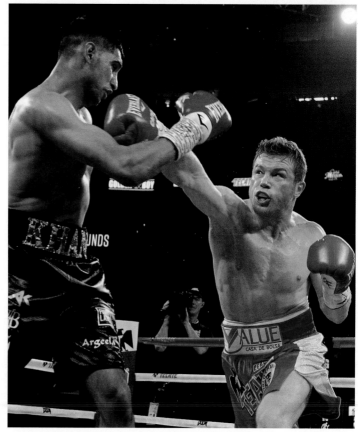

When I took out the former WBA welterweight champion Luis Collazo (*above*) at the MGM Grand in Las Vegas in May 2014, making a mockery of his hands-down technique by putting him on the floor three times, and then (December 2014) totally overwhelmed Devon Alexander (*below*) at the same venue – in a pair of shorts with a 24-carat gold thread waistband no less – I really felt like I'd earned my place back at the top table.

April 2019 against Terence Crawford. I've never been nervous walking out for a fight. If anything, I've always revelled in the spotlight. I love the whole razzmatazz – lights flashing, music blaring, compère bigging the whole thing up, crowd going mad . . . But Madison Square Garden was different level.

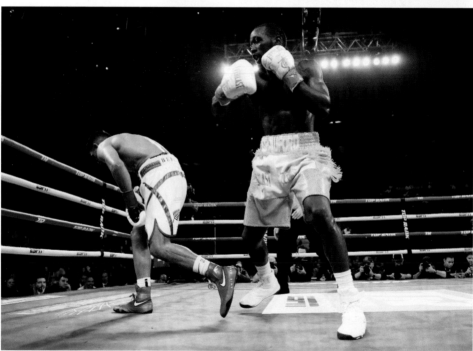

I'm gasping for air. Drowning. I force open my eyes and remember, through the bright lights and the blurs, that I'm in Madison Square Garden . . . I've just been hit by a low blow from Terence Crawford. It feels like I've taken a cannonball in the shorts.

I didn't see Faryal as just another girl. She was special and even at the start I couldn't help thinking she was someone I'd love to marry. I think I might even have mentioned she was marriage material because later she said she thought I was a 'total bullshitter'!

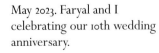

May 2023. Faryal and I celebrating our 10th wedding anniversary.

Miracles do happen — look at my marriage! Who'd have thought that would have survived — at times me and Faryal have definitely reached number nine of a ten count — and we're still here.

2014. My parents meeting our first-born child Lamaisah.

In Lockdown 2021. With our son Zaviyar on his first birthday.

May 2023. With our daughters Lamaisah (*left*) and Alayna (*right*).

didn't really know his style, what type of fighter he was. Don't get me wrong, I could have done more myself on that front, but any boxer will tell you how important it is to have a team who nail that stuff on your behalf and make sure you know precisely what you're coming up against. I was on the floor after fifty-four seconds so clearly they didn't do a good job on that. As one of my all-time heroes Mike Tyson once said: 'Everybody has a plan until they get punched in the mouth.' I didn't even have that.

As the days passed, more and more people began to put the boot in. According to who you listened to I was either arrogant and had it coming or was just another flash in the pan. I was being compared to gone-in-sixty-seconds fighters from the past I'd never heard of. Prescott, from the back streets of Barranquilla, the pundits said, wanted it more than the upstart with his comfortable life in Bolton.

Frank, at least, was fighting my corner. As annoyed as I was that Prescott had been put in front of me, and frustrated with himself for not resisting Rubio's advice, he bigged me up as an entertainer, a risk-taker, and someone who'd soon be back on the track to world titles. While promoters have to say that sort of stuff, Frank's words helped. I began to get more philosophical. Being positive is my default position and even though Prescott was a hard defeat to take, I slowly started looking at it like this – things happen for a reason. I was an emerging pro, not the finished product, and losing to Prescott was all part of that learning curve – maybe a part better learned now than later, a reminder that the world I was in no longer consisted of pushovers but proper hard men.

I also came to see the defeat as a pressure release. In many ways my star had risen too early. Since the age of seventeen I'd been treated in the same way – the attention and the praise – you'd expect a world champion to be treated. Except in my case I'd not won a world title, I'd won an Olympic silver medal. I wanted as much as anyone to show people I was the real deal but maybe expectations had been too high too early. I knew I had plenty of time to come back. I'd had losses in my amateur career and done exactly that. This was just another blip. I would return better and stronger. Maybe losing to Prescott wasn't a curse but a blessing.

I also wanted to take the heat off my camp – Rubio, Frank, my family, everyone. Lose and people soon start clawing at one another, trying to shift the blame from their own door. I tried to make it nice and easy. 'I'm the one to blame,' I told them. 'I'm the one who lost the fight, so please don't blame anyone else.' I was happy to do that to stop any bitching or in-fighting. I might not have been the finished article as a boxer but I was definitely wiser and smarter than I had been a few days before.

I concluded that, one way or another, losing a pro fight at some point was only to be expected. What was less expected was how that loss sparked a mass exodus of those who I thought of as my allies. I'd heard people say that in sport you soon find out who your friends are when the tide turns. Even so, I hadn't expected it to happen so quickly. I mean, one defeat?

Friends, from both the English and Asian communities, disappeared overnight, as did some of those on my team. For them the polish had come off. They could no longer see their reflection in my glory. Suddenly phones went to message instead of immediately being picked up. Fellow fighters, who previously couldn't wait to tell everyone how I was the next big thing, started talking shit, putting me down, saying I was a done deal. 'I knew it was going to happen,' they'd say. 'I saw how he used to train – he wasn't as good as people made out.' It made them feel more important to pretend they knew the inside story of why it had all gone so horribly wrong. It made me think of some of the documentaries I'd seen about Tyson where fighter after fighter lined up to say something bad about him. *Well, it's on TV*, I'd think, *so it must be true*. Now it was happening to me and I could see how some people just can't wait to have a microphone shoved in their face

93

and talk bollocks about you. Sport is fickle. People want to be around you when you're winning. Make one mistake and they're gone.

. . .

Prescott described the fight as 'the biggest moment of my life'. In many ways, it was the biggest of mine as well. While I felt my career could and would be rescued, I couldn't help but notice something really disturbing going on. The minute I lost that fight, a real undercurrent of something dark began to boil up – something that would eventually go a long way to me quitting the country.

While I was flying high in the early days of my pro career, everyone was behind me. On a wider scale, the country was also coming to terms with the spectre of Islamic terrorism. By speaking openly about the issue and wrapping myself in the Union Jack, I'd tried to be a voice of unity. Once I lost to Prescott, all that was thrown back in my face. Racism might always have been bubbling under the surface but now it came bursting out. Win and people happily accepted me as British. Lose and I was Pakistani.

Some of my English 'friends' said to me: 'You're just a typical Asian.' I even had it from people in the Pakistani community. They'd been waiting for me to slip up and couldn't wait to mock me for my actions. 'You're shit,' I'd be told. 'Keep flying that British flag. Lot of good it's done you.' It wasn't even jealousy. It was pure happiness that I'd been beaten.

It took a lot of mental strength to get past that. People jabbing at me with their views. At the end of the day, I'm a fighter. I'm not going to let someone say something to me, put me down. But I knew as well as they did that I couldn't retaliate. Give someone a good hiding and I'd lose everything, including my future. It got to the stage where I stopped going out in case someone tried to push my buttons.

It was there in the media too. Some writers started showing their true colours, saying the 'Asian fighter' Amir Khan was a busted flush. I was upset that people had turned against me. I tried not to let it affect me emotionally. I knew if I really dwelt on it, it could destroy me. Despite what some might think, I'm a very humble person, something which, in the ultimate big-yourself-up sport, people don't always see. Maybe that's why I do sometimes let things get to me. They upset me more than people understand. I'm the opposite of who they think I am.

Part of what kept me going, not just then but throughout my career, was the love I got from Pakistan.

One of the best things my dad did was give the broadcasting rights for my fights to Pakistan for nothing, just to generate some interest, no matter how small, in boxing. Initially, the TV people said even for free they didn't want to show it – 'No one likes boxing,' was all we heard. And it's true, you have to go all the way back to the heyday of Muhammad Ali for anyone in Pakistan to be bothered about the sport. Even then it was mainly because of Ali's Muslim faith. We tried to emphasise the significance of myself as a British Pakistani, but still they wouldn't listen.

Eventually, as my fights got bigger and bigger, they came round to the idea, and my bouts became a massive hit. The same TV companies that had turned them down for free were now fighting to buy my rights. I went from complete anonymity to it feeling like the entire country knew who I was. I was lit up on billboards and on TV commercials seen by millions. Even now if I go to Pakistan the streets are packed with people wanting to see me. The police and army have had to develop protocols for when I visit. That might sound a bit over the top, but Pakistan is an unstable country. If I unknowingly head into an unpredictable area, anything can happen. I tend to be around the British ambassador, and he always insists I have security in case, God forbid, something happens. He always wants to make sure I'm safe and I'm massively grateful to the security services for making sure I'm OK.

Nothing ever has gone wrong, and I've never felt anything but love. An incredible, incredible, place.

At times of crisis, the support of the Pakistani people would always help me rebuild my confidence. 'I'm doing it for them,' I'd tell myself. 'I'm not even doing it for myself. I'm doing it for the millions who are watching me and cry and pray for me. I've got real love from these people and I'm not going to let the negativity get on top of me.'

To feel that huge love at a time when everything else feels like it's shrinking around you is something else. It always made me wonder why skin colour is such a big thing in Britain, why some people couldn't see past my heritage. It wasn't reported on much at the time but my family had been given a rough time in the arena after the Prescott defeat. There'd been pushing, shoving, abuse hurled. It wound me up and I did actually come out and say it one interview – 'I know if I was a white English fighter I would be a superstar in Britain and the world.'

That might have been a bit over the top but it did have a ring of truth about it. For those with prejudice in their bones I would always be unworthy of their praise. Whether that came from jealousy of my achievements or something worse, I don't know. But it did feel there were people out there using my Muslim faith to create ill-feeling against me. There wasn't much I could do about that other than try to put it to the back of my mind, made easier because people, like the keyboard warriors who'd soon pop up on social media, would never make a blatantly racist remark to my face. I suppose that's one benefit of being able to knock people out!

As the British National Party began to make gains across the north-west, including Bolton, its leader, Nick Griffin, said I should be 'encouraged' to leave Britain. 'Perhaps we will lose one good boxer,' he said, 'but there are more important things.' As someone born in Great Britain who, unlike him, had won a medal for my country I found his comments a little bit puzzling. It was the usual twisting of who people with Pakistani heritage are. We're English, we're British, but that connection with Pakistan will always be there. It's where our parents, our grandparents, come from. That's why when Pakistan play cricket against England it's insane. But that doesn't mean we aren't loyal to Britain. I wore Union Jack colours in the ring, as an amateur and a professional, many times. Don't forget, I could just as easily have won that Olympic medal for Pakistan, or even the USA! It's not just Pakistan, Lewis Hamilton's dad is of Grenadian descent. Does that mean Lewis should be slung out of the country too?

I've always respected other people's religions — prejudice isn't part of my life — and I find it sad that other people can't do the same. I've also refused to let prejudice against myself weaken me in any way. Yes it can hurt, but whenever I hear negativity it always drives me to be a stronger person. Sticks and stones and all that. I could never force people to accept me but what I could do is make sure it never diverted me from my path. I always tried to remember it was just a few people doing all the shouting. Everyone else wanted me to do well and was happy for me to get on with it.

. . .

Whatever the madness of prejudice, back in the world of boxing I did understand one thing was obvious – I couldn't stick with Rubio. It wasn't that he was a bad coach, it was more that we'd hit a red light before we'd even started. A loss to someone like Prescott was too damaging to continue as if nothing had happened. The defeat had broken the relationship. Prescott was Rubio's call and it had backfired horribly. I needed a coach who could teach me how to reach the next level – and this time actually make it.

More than that, I needed something new. I needed to get the love back. The Prescott fight had left me searching for a kick-start, something totally new in my life. Its aftermath had left a bitter taste. It was something I wanted to wash right out of my mouth.

99

My mind began turning to America, the continent where so many of the big names I respected came from. I'd been out there a couple of years earlier. I'd visited Gleason's Gym in New York, backdrop to the careers of some of the absolute greats of world boxing, including Roberto Duran, Rocky Graziano and none other than Muhammad Ali. Crazily, on that trip I'd actually flown to meet the great man at his home in Louisville, Kentucky. It remains, as you'd expect, one of the best moments of my life. I actually sat and spoke with Ali for an hour. Sadly, his speech had deteriorated at this point because of his Parkinson's, but he laughed, hugged me and held my hand. He even gave me a pair of autographed shorts, which obviously I still have, along with a treasured picture of me and him on that day.

One thing that struck me from that visit to Kentucky was there seemed to be a lot more respect shown for the KFC founder Colonel Sanders than there was for Ali. I expected there to be much more of a celebration of this local hero, but there was virtually nothing. Maybe his achievements didn't mean so much there. I don't just mean his boxing, but what he did for the civil rights and anti-war movements. I don't know whether that's the case but I do know Ali is a hero to every Muslim. He was definitely a hero to me.

Thanks to people like Ali, America seemed somewhere

it was easy to be yourself. I was no expert but it felt like a place you could just get on with life. I liked the thought of walking into a gym in Los Angeles and being a total stranger – at most, someone clocking me, giving me a nod of the head, and that being the end of it. In the early days at least, I could have a different life there. I'd think about how I'd wake at six in the morning and go for a run, nobody looking at me, nobody really knowing me. Attention's OK – until it isn't. Going to America would take all the pressure away from me. I'd get away from everything, not be seen as Amir Khan the Olympic boxer, and start again.

I've never really stopped and thought about this before, but I get it now – I wanted to be left alone. That's why I went to America – to be left alone.

COACHING SESSION 4

They say if you've got a hundred messages on your phone, ninety-nine of them are positive and one is negative, it's the negative one you remember. There was a time when I'd have said that's true – but I didn't feel like that for long.

I soon realised that some people will always be a waste of time and energy. That's just the way it is. I faced prejudice because of my heritage. You might face prejudice for other reasons. People who hate want to get under your skin. Don't let them. Block them, cut them out of your life, and listen to the positive voices. They're the ones that matter, and they're the ones who'll carry you to bigger and better things.

ROUND FIVE

I made contact with Freddie Roach, a big-name trainer who looked after Manny Pacquiao, a pound-for-pound legend whose style made him one of the most exciting fighters on the planet. Like millions of others I couldn't get enough of watching him.

With my next outing, against the Irishman Oisin Fagan in London, just three months away we didn't waste any time. Freddie invited me to spend a weekend at his renowned Wild Card gym in Los Angeles before confirming a six-week block of training in the run-up to the fight. There were a few nerves of course but overall I had little trepidation about upping sticks and heading over there. You have to take a leap if you want to reach the next stage.

Contacting Freddie was one of the best moves I ever made. If you're the main man in a gym it can happen, subconsciously more than anything, that you don't push yourself. Familiarity and routine lead to boredom. You don't always feel stimulated. But when you're in a gym and you've got the ultra-tough Filipino multi-world champion Manny Pacquiao there, one of the best fighters in the world, as well as a trainer like Freddie, you want to work harder than ever to show them you belong in their company.

Straight away at the Wild Card I liked what I saw. This place was definitely no-frills. You entered down a set of back steps by a laundry. The rest of the street was a mix of fast-food joints and Manny's tattoo parlour! Manny was covered in ink and obviously thought it would be cheaper just to buy a shop for himself! The gym itself looked like it hadn't seen a lick of paint for years. It was a proper place where people came to work hard, not just the pros but blokes who walked in off the street – for just five dollars anyone could come through the doors. Right from day one that atmosphere brought the best out in me. It was tough but I enjoyed every minute of it.

Freddie wouldn't actually be present in London because the Fagan fight clashed with the meeting of Manny and Oscar De La Hoya in Las Vegas. Billed as 'The Dream Match', I could see it was a slightly bigger battle than mine!

Freddie hadn't reached such heights without knowing exactly how to make the most of every boxer in his charge. He saw in me a fighter who was feeling lost and uncertain after taking a big confidence blow. He didn't have time to make full-scale changes but what he did do was really talk up the positives about my ability and style. He taught me that desire was good, but only if it was backed up by solid unbeatable skill. Freddie knew how to use the mind as well as the body. At one point someone asked him if Manny had been helped by sparring with me (unbelievably this was actually a thing). Freddie's response was that my jab was better than De La Hoya's and if Manny could deal with that then he could deal with anything. If he said that to boost my confidence, then it worked. He made me feel good about myself and reassured me that losing to a fighter at Prescott's level couldn't happen again.

That self-esteem boost was multiplied by the change in lifestyle and culture that surrounded me in the States. I loved what I saw in LA, soaking up the natural positivity and using it to my advantage in my training. Fagan was duly stopped in the second round (later it was discovered he'd actually broken his ankle when I knocked him down in the first) and I could start training with Freddie properly.

It really did feel like I'd landed somewhere that could, and would, make me a champion, launch me into the big time. Just watching Manny, whose work rate and attitude was like no other fighter I'd been near, was incredible. I knew if they'd got so much out of him they could get it out of me as well. Freddie was a man who saw my key attributes – speed, power, agility – and knew straight away how to make the best of them.

After Fagan it was important to get me fighting big

names again. That way I'd quickly rebuild my reputation as a force to be reckoned with and get rid of any lingering self-belief issues post-Prescott. A fight in Manchester with Marco Antonio Barrera was scheduled, again in just three months' time, with the World Boxing Association (WBA) International lightweight and WBO Inter-Continental lightweight titles on the line.

When Barrera's name was first mentioned all I could think of was how the Mexican had convincingly outfought Prince Naseem eight years before, the only loss of Naseem's pro career and a fight I'd stayed up half the night with my mates to watch. I'd just come off one of the worst losses of my career, to pretty much a complete nobody, so I think I can be forgiven for having a few doubts. Everyone in the media seemed to think it would be an easy fight but, like all Mexican boxers, Barrera's passion made him a formidable opponent. He might now have been in his mid-thirties but, no disrespect to Fagan, he'd be a different test altogether. He was a gnarled and wily veteran of this road, a smart and clever fighter who had been stopped only once in a sixty-four-fight career and remained the number one ranked lightweight with the WBO. I'm sure Barrera would have looked at me as vulnerable after a defeat and still pretty new to the professional game. It was Khan versus Barrera, but it was basically youth versus experience.

While most people did expect me to see off Barrera, the fight was a good illustration of the risks I was willing to take to make up the ground lost due to the Prescott debacle. At any one time, there's no shortage of boxers scrabbling for the next rung on the ladder and in losing to Prescott I'd landed on a snake. As I slipped back, they trod on my hands as they carried on past. You can either try to make up that ground slowly or you can take a riskier path. If it comes off, all's good. You're a contender again. Your promoter's happy because the money's good and the TV companies are happy because they've got big-audience fights. Lose again and you're back to square one. It's a classic catch-22 situation – a promoter has to protect his investment but at the same time must put it at risk to earn the big money.

Even Frank admitted he was nervous when it came to Barrera but I needed a big-name fight to put me back up where I needed to be. Beat any fighter and the minimum it does is put you one above him. Barrera was a rankings-topper, a proper legend of the sport. Beat him and I'd be right in the mix for world titles. There was one other thing that drew me to Barrera – I liked the thought of getting revenge for Naseem who, at that time, was a friend of mine.

As my career progressed, I would always take these risky fights. Most times it worked. I stepped out of the casino with pockets bulging to the sound of birds singing and bright sunshine. Other times it was dark, raining, I was skint, and my car wouldn't start! Barrera was a birds-and-sunshine type of occasion. Me and Freddie had worked him out good and proper. Barrera was not your classic all-guns-blazing kind of character. He preferred to sit back, be patient, and await his chance. That's OK, it works for a lot of boxers, but we knew my speed in the ring wouldn't allow him to relax. We wouldn't give him a spare second. I had also made a point of sparring with guys who specialised in the counter-attack, who try to get you cornered. And, yes, of course, we'd worked out a good defence against a Prescott-like haymaker.

The plan worked well. I was dominating Barrera – my youth really did make a difference – and he ran out of steam before a cut to his head saw the ref stop the fight in round five. Don King, one of the biggest, most controversial and instantly recognisable faces in the boxing business – his bush of frizzy grey hair streaked with white was a legend in itself – was Barrera's promoter and went to war on his behalf. He claimed the cut to Barrera's head meant the fight should have been abandoned. Don was a hard man to ignore – his past fights included the 'Rumble in the Jungle' and down the years he'd promoted everyone from Larry Holmes to Mike Tyson and Evander Holyfield – but on this occasion his nonsense fell on deaf ears. The cut had come from a clash of heads. It was just one of those things. I had beaten Barrera fair and square. My speed had done for him and he'd looked lumbering in comparison.

It was a landmark win, not least because it was my first back at the MEN Arena since the Prescott defeat had turned ugly. At first, as I made my way to the ring, it seemed that an unpleasant aftertaste from that fight remained. If anything, it felt like Barrera was the home fighter as his appearance prompted some pretty wild cheers. Even through the dazzle of the spotlights I could see that anyone selling Mexican sombreros outside the arena had made a killing. I think that was more in the party spirit, a great Manchester welcome for a boxing superstar like Barrera, than anything against me. And while there were a few boos, they stopped as soon as people saw I was there to put on a class performance and show that Prescott was a blip and I was back to my best. I even took a couple of shots on the chin that was now regularly being described as dodgy by those who, it felt, almost wanted me to fail. After one such shot I even threw my arms in the air to illustrate it was no big deal. After the massive down of Prescott, all I felt on the Barrera night was massive exhilaration; like a new improved me doing the thing I love. Freddie agreed. 'He'll be my next world champion,' he told the media. 'I have no doubt about that.'

As for Don King, he had vowed before the fight to visit Bolton to see 'where a guy like Amir Khan comes from'. 'The people there have got to be great and gracious,' he said. He was right about that – but he never turned up.

. . .

I returned to LA floating on air. I could hardly believe the shift in fortunes I'd experienced in such a short time. Being around Manny in particular was a massive thing for me. We'd run together – I was one of the few people who could keep up with him! – and, between gasps for air, we'd talk. In some ways I could see a mirror between me and him. Manny too had been written off after an early knockout in his career but had come back to be one of the biggest names in world boxing. He was generous in his advice and being around him gave me a big confidence lift. We became really close and it meant a lot to me that he respected me as a training partner. It's stupid, I know, but one time we went for a run and afterwards, when I realised I didn't have my water, he gave me his. It was a little thing but it showed how caring he was. Whatever the other one did or achieved, there was never any jealousy, something which can so easily happen when sportspeople are forced together. Look at the average football dressing room.

A lot of that mutual respect was built on having similar backgrounds. We might have grown up thousands of miles apart geographically and culturally but we had both been brought up to respect family and help other people. It sounds a bit crap I know, but we both had good hearts. It was like we knew you don't have to be a bad guy all the time to be a good boxer, or to achieve anything else in life. We actually liked being the good guys, maybe again because we'd come from families who'd seen struggle but had never been short of love. It was shared values that made us so close. The only shame was that throughout our long careers we never quite managed to get it together in the ring. There was talk at various points but, as happens sometimes, the timing was never quite right.

With Barrera dispatched, there was talk of a rematch with Prescott. While it would have been nice to show once and for all that the knockout had been a fluke, it would have been a waste of my position. I had a proven pedigree. I had a good following. I had a well-known name. And I had Frank Warren.

Frank sorted a showdown with the Ukrainian, Andreas Kotelnik. At stake was the WBA light-welterweight title. Here, at last, it was – the world title fight I'd dreamed about. The venue, again, would be the MEN Arena in Manchester. Kotelnik, as his world champion status suggested, was never going to be a pushover. Last time out he'd defended his title against the tough Argentine, Marcos Maidana. I'd been expected to beat Barrera but the outcome against Kotelnik was never going to be so clear-cut, especially bearing in mind this would be my first outing at light-welterweight rather than lightweight, but I was confident I had the beating of him. I'd had a good few months around Freddie and Manny by now. I was twice the boxer I'd been a year previously.

The night itself had a different feel to the Barrera fight. While that had a kind of 'big night out' atmosphere, the crowd seemed to recognise that this time round there was more at stake. If everything went to plan, five years after the local lad went to Athens and came back with silver they'd be watching him fulfil a dream of becoming world champion.

Kotelnik was a guy who could soak up punches and pressure and so it was always going to be a long night. I knew my concentration had to be spot on and my challenge was to keep the hand speed high, get my feet moving, keep landing punches, and not rush in. As the last round started, the crowd were celebrating the win; my family were on their feet. That's an amazing feeling and one which makes me shiver even now. I knew they were right. I'd totally out-fought Kotelnik. The challenge for me was not to get carried away. See out those three minutes and my dream would come true.

When the unanimous verdict was announced, I looked round, trying to take it all in, to create the memory. I thanked God, I thanked my family, and I thanked Freddie. Three fights since I'd been flat out on that canvas staring into space at what could have been the wreck of my career, I was now being hoisted aloft by my corner while the WBA belt was wrapped round my waist. Unbelievable.

There was another thing about that win, something that was maybe more apparent to me than others – I was the only Muslim world champion. As such I became massively visible to other Muslims around the world and began to get loads of fans, not just in the obvious countries like India and Pakistan, but unexpected places such as Iraq, Lebanon and Dubai. People would send me recordings of commentaries of my fights where I had no idea what language was being spoken or even what country it was coming from. Same with magazine articles. The only reason I knew they were about me was because my picture was splashed all over them. It wasn't just boxing that fans were interested in, they wanted to know everything I was getting up to as a person. Being Asian, being different, was definitely a huge help to my profile. Although when I stopped to think about it, I couldn't help but think how mad it all was. There were people thousands of miles away in countries I knew nothing about following my career. That kind of thing can make your head hurt if you're not careful!

. . .

Being a world champion felt like a line in the sand. In many ways, time for a new start. The New Yorker Dmitriy Salita, in Newcastle, was my launch point. A seventy-six-second demolition, it was notable more for being the first time a Jew and a Muslim had fought for a world title than anything that happened in the ring. You can imagine the kind of big deal people wanted to make of the religious aspect but neither of us was interested. There was no animosity. We are still friends to this day.

Soon after I was approached again by Oscar De La Hoya's Golden Boy Promotions. Oscar felt he could help me make more breakthroughs into boxing Stateside. While I'd been training a lot in the US I really wanted to be fighting and building my fan base there too. Oscar, recently retired after proving himself one of the all-time greats of the sport, came to see me train. He wanted to be part of me. It was funny – because I'd been on his radar for a good while, he'd talk to me like he knew me. It didn't take me long to make up my mind. I could see he believed in me massively and would do everything in his power to get me the biggest fights out there.

Of course, there was the little matter of Frank Warren. Having been alongside me during my rise to world champion he was unlikely to be leaping for joy. As predicted, Frank branded me disloyal for making the move. He was a big name already but maybe he thought he needed someone like myself to then become really massive. I'd made him a lot of money, and obviously he'd helped to make me a big name as well, but in boxing, as in any sport, a good pro will always run towards anyone who they think is better equipped to take them to the next stage. The much easier thing to do is stick with what you know.

Thankfully, as well as my own thoughts, I always had my family there to help make the tough decisions. They never relinquished control and so were permanently in the driving seat. They had a 360-degree view of my career all the time. Without them, like so many other boxers, I'd have been wandering through that minefield of boxing promotion on my own, trying to pick out the good advice from the bad, the sharks from those who genuinely had my best interests at heart.

It's scary for young boxers. Often they sign up to a promoter and find themselves wasting the best years of their careers. Some promoters might even threaten to end your career if you go with someone else. They use fear to keep you in their grasp. 'Stick with me,' they say, 'or you'll never get a big fight.' What's really shocking is that trainers are now asking young fighters to do the same. Locking naive kids into these awful suffocating deals, making sure they can't go anywhere, effectively becoming a manager as well as a trainer, is becoming a business for these people.

Only yesterday I was talking to a young kid who was telling me about his career. I was worried for him because I know there are those out there who will exploit him if he's not careful. 'Don't sign a long-term deal,' I told him. 'Don't lock yourself in with someone. Don't listen when they say you have to be with them to get the best opportunities. Look at all the trainers out there – the best will never ask you to do that.'

I totally get why that whole world of deals and promoters can seem so terrifying from the outside. People get shot. It does happen. And somewhere behind all that nonsense there'll be fighters who thought they were getting a six-figure sum for a fight, maybe more, and ending up with twenty grand. They can complain but it will be hidden away somewhere in a contract. They probably should have read that contract better, but maybe they found it too technical. Or they might have got a good lawyer to go over it, except they couldn't afford it. With my dad taking control of the business side of operations I never had any of that. Dad started off in the world of boxing the same time as me, but he soon learned. He's smart like that. No matter how big the circles we were mixing in, he had the best business head. We were never going to get shafted. Unlike so many others, I never once found myself in shark-infested waters.

It was a pity what happened with Frank but at the end of the day it was business. I'm sure he's made a few unpopular decisions himself. These days we're all fine again, and I'm pleased about that. I've never forgotten how in those early years he was by my side.

Oscar wasted no time bigging me up. He described me as 'charismatic and outgoing'. I don't care who you are or what you do that's always going to be nice to hear! On a more serious note, he also noted that there was work to do if I was to truly fulfil my potential.

'One thing about Amir Khan,' he reflected, 'is he's sometimes a little too brave for his own good. People might say that that's been his Achilles' heel.' No matter how hard he or anyone else tried, that heel would never quite be fixed.

Golden Boy knew that my first outing in America needed to be a spectacle, a chance for me to show a whole new audience what I was about and what I could do. The result was a fight at Madison Square Garden against Paulie Malignaggi, a former International Boxing Federation (IBF) light-welterweight champion who had been beaten by Ricky Hatton two years earlier. Malignaggi was known as a guy who didn't give up easily. In England he was also remembered for his trainer cutting off his hair extensions in a fight against Lovemore N'dou at the City of Manchester Stadium! Oscar knew that fighting Malignaggi in a big city like New York would be a great way to build a fan base. At that time, I was thinking more towards Las Vegas, but if you think about it the desert city is more of a boxing venue than somewhere to build a following. Oscar wanted to create something long-lasting. He had a good head like that.

Throughout my career, my fan base across the Atlantic was always a fascinating thing. I obviously had a big Asian following in America but what was funny was all the Mexicans who liked me. I'm pretty sure that was because Freddie virtually turned me into a Mexican fighter rather than them thinking I looked Mexican! Either way I always had them behind me, even if I had beaten the local hero Barrera and pinched his crown.

I was never in trouble against Malignaggi, although, as expected, he somehow hung in there until the referee stopped the fight as I laid into him on the ropes in the eleventh round. For me, the test had not been so much the fight as everything that went with it – my first fight in America, my first with a new promoter. That kind of difference isn't to be sniffed at. I've seen guys who have been to America for the first time and struggled. Just look at what happened to Anthony Joshua. First time he fights in America he loses to a 25/1 outsider. When you're used to things being done in a certain way, the slightest change can knock you. It can be a bigger threat than the guy in the opposite corner. It creates a different kind of pressure. Luckily, I got through it, but it could have finished my career.

Again it all came down to risk. If I was going to be a boxer, I wanted to make sure I was going to be different. I wanted to bring something new to the sport in the way I'd seen Muhammad Ali and Naseem Hamed do it. For me that 'something' was my speed, it was my footwork. But it was also my desire, unlike most British fighters, to go to America early in my career. In no way was that move guaranteed to work. It could have been a big mistake. I could have gone to America and got beat in my first fight, at which point people would have quickly forgotten about me. Equally, a move away from the UK might have been seen as arrogant and alienated my fans.

I knew also that if I was to carry on being among people like Freddie and Manny, I had to be successful. I had to keep on winning. That meant not being carried away by distractions – of which there were many.

• • •

My apartment was just off the famed Sunset Boulevard, with, among others, Snoop Dogg as a neighbour. He would often pop in for a chat about boxing, which he knew nothing about – 'Is this sport for real?' It made me laugh when a few years ago he piped up that he was starting his own boxing league with himself as commentator and announcer.

Other times I'd make the ten-minute walk down to the gym and next thing I knew the hardman actor Jason Statham would walk in to see me train. Not to see Manny Pacquiao train, but to see me. Manny would be looking at him – 'I was just watching your movie!' Mark Wahlberg, preparing for a lead role in *The Fighter*, playing a boxer seeking the big time, actually came to train with me so he had an idea how to look right in the part. Vinnie Jones, maybe looking to build on his already pretty convincing hardman act, might also pop in, along with Mickey Rourke, who had been a fearsome amateur fighter in his time, at one point knocking out twelve fighters in a row. Maybe it should have been me watching him! Mario Lopez, known across the globe from the US sitcom *Saved by the Bell*, was another big-name actor always in the gym, while Lennox Lewis would come along to watch me spar and say hello. Often I'd be invited out for dinner by some celebrity or other at some fancy restaurant. I was a professional sportsman on a strict routine but when you've got Hollywood A-listers asking you to dinner it's not easy to say no.

I'd be lying if I said you can't get carried away, go off the rails even, in that environment. The parties, the celebrities, the women – it's a combination that can quickly lead you astray. Take your eye off what it is that got you there in the first place, and before you know it it's disappeared. I was very young when success came my way. Olympic silver medallist at seventeen, world champion at twenty-two. I was doing the rounds of the big talk shows in America not that long after I was giving interviews to *The Bolton News*.

I had to be disciplined. It would have been very easy to get ahead of myself. I was young, a world champion. I'd be getting invites to all these crazy events at famous nightclubs. Everywhere I looked there'd be people the likes of me only ever normally see on TV shows or at the movies. I'll be straight with you, I loved it. I consider myself humble, but for me to be invited to these places, to meet these kinds of people, was amazing. True to say, though, that over time I would come to see it all in a totally different way.

There was something else I noticed about America. There they celebrated success. It felt like their sporting heroes were genuinely loved, not just there to be set up and shot down. I couldn't help but compare that attitude to how quickly some people in the UK had turned on me after that defeat to Prescott. In America it just felt like everyone wanted to shake my hand and tell me how much they liked watching me and what a great job I was doing. They liked the fact I'd got up off my 'ass' after Prescott and done something about it. In Britain, too many people had told me I was finished. By going to America to fight I knew I could become a superstar.

Without making that move, I'd probably have been pretty anonymous over there. Now it doesn't matter where I go in America, whatever state, people know who Amir Khan is. It still shocks me. Not long ago I was in Omaha, Nebraska, training for my last fight. I've never been there before, and yet people were coming up to me and saying: 'Wow! You're the boxer – Amir Khan!' The same thing happened when I went up in the mountains to Colorado Springs. I'd never even heard of Colorado Springs! But they'd heard of me. That's what going to America, fighting over there, did for me. It created such a big fan base. To be successful, a fighter who is known, is what I wanted all my life. And America is where I lived that dream. Freddie had promised me that basing myself in America would change everything and he wasn't wrong. It was the big turning point in my career – the point I really went from 'the Kid' to the man.

As ever, my parents would always keep my feet on the ground. They would often visit, my mum's cooking being a massive treat for someone never keen to spend too much time in the kitchen. But perspective had an awful habit of coming from elsewhere too. Again, Pakistan was hit by disaster in 2010. This time devastating floods made millions homeless, and again I went out to help Oxfam distribute aid. Seeing people with absolutely nothing trying desperately to survive is a great way to make you realise who are the real fighters in life. When I got home I organised a Bollywood-themed dinner in Bolton to raise money to rebuild eight schools washed away by the floodwater. I was blessed to be living the life I was and felt that, since God had built this platform for me, I should do everything to use it in the best way I possibly could. I also thought again of the incredible backing the people of Pakistan had given me. All through my career I was desperate to be there for them and that would always provide massive motivation to keep working hard.

Working with Freddie, motivation would never be lacking. I'd had no doubts about going with him, but within just a few months he really had confirmed to me he was the best coach in the world. The leading trainers don't just see the fighter, they see the person. Their brilliance is in combining the two. Rather than keep their distance they want to get in your head, to man-manage you, because they know two fighters are never the same. A coach can't just say: 'You've got to train for twelve hours, get on with it.' That might work for one person but it could never work for everybody.

Freddie had obviously learned so much from his own experience of being a fighter, not just in the ring but his relationships with coaches, and wanted to turn that knowhow into being the best around. Just looking at what Freddie had achieved with Manny gave me the confidence that his approach was the right one. Manny was similar to me in many ways – an ambitious and single-minded character whose success was based on speed, movement and aggression. What Freddie did was work with Manny's talent and personality to create a finished article that was absolutely the best it could be. He tried to do exactly the same with me – to create a fighter who would need someone really special to come along and beat me. To make me into one of the very best offensive fighters in the world.

And in that he totally succeeded. I had entered my greatest phase.

COACHING SESSION 5

Never be afraid of the big move. Never put it off. Never waste time asking if it will work. Why? Because before you know it the chance will be gone.

On the face of it, I was a lad from Bolton. That's where my life should always have been. But I had a talent that took me to the other side of the globe. The beauty of the world now is that no one has to feel stuck in one place. Doesn't matter what you're good at, opportunity is out there – you just have to take it. I know people will think 'that's easy for him to say'. But it's true. We live in a small world, and trying different countries, different cultures, isn't the big deal it once was. You can always come back to your roots if that's what you want.

In life, you only regret what you've never done.

ROUND SIX

It would be the toughest fight of my life. The one that defined me then, and the one I hope will define me for years to come. The deepest I ever had to dig to get over the line.

Marcos Maidana was a guy I'd seen beating opponents up, knocking everyone out. The Argentine was a big puncher, a dangerous guy. One of those fighters who just keeps coming at you all the time so you never get the chance to reset. You're lucky if you can even take a breath. I hated fighting people like that.

To say Maidana was a danger man was the understatement of the year. All but two of his wins had come from stoppages. This would be either a really big ladder or a very long snake. I'll be straight, there were times in the run-up to that fight where I was thinking *Oh fuck!* But I had to do it. I was cornered. Maidana was the mandatory challenger. He couldn't be swerved.

From Golden Boy's point of view it was a great match-up. They just wanted to see an exciting fight. They were right from that point of view – pitching two boxers on fire against each other is always going to make for a memorable night. Freddie Roach, on the other hand, was less pleased. From his point of view it was a big risk me putting my hard-earned light-welterweight world title on the line against a monstrous hitter like Maidana when I was still establishing myself at the top table.

The boxing press would constantly throw petrol on that particular fire. In the run-up to the clash, again and again they put me down. 'He can't take a punch. He's got a glass chin.' I heard it so often that it began actually to infest my mind. 'Am I really that type of fighter?' The more people say something, the more you end up believing it. I'm only human. I'd seen Maidana knock out guys who had a very good chin, who'd never been down before. I consoled myself that this was another chance to dispel the myth. I knew also that Maidana's defence was far from perfect. As one commentator put it: 'Maidana gets hit more often than a windshield does with gnats on a cross-country drive.'

The fight was scheduled for the Mandalay Bay resort in Las Vegas. With my first US fight out the way, and New York firmly on my side, it was time to make some waves in the biggest boxing city of them all. Nothing can ever really rival that moment when you see your name up in lights on the famous Strip, that crazy epicentre of casinos, hotels and venues where the biggest names in entertainment have performed down the years. As a boxer I never took these moments for granted and vowed to keep them all in my memory bank. There would be times when all this was ancient history and it would be great to look back – I think even then I was indulging that fantasy of sitting with grandkids on my knee telling them of my greatest escapades. There would also be times in my career when the attention of the boxing world shifted elsewhere, times when thinking about big moments like this would be a welcome boost.

It was amazing to see that people had travelled from the UK to support me. In the days leading up to the fight I must have seen the shirts of half the Football League wandering round Vegas. I just hoped I'd be able to give them something to shout about.

Thankfully, early on against Maidana things were going about as well as they ever could. I caught him with a devastatingly clean body shot to the liver. His face, tied up in an ugly grimace, said everything. To me, that punch came from God. I might well have lost that fight without it, but instead I was gifted a moment that saved me. That blow didn't just give me confidence, it slowed him. Putting someone down with a body shot is like popping a balloon, except in this case it's energy not air that instantly escapes. That single punch took away his legs, his power and his breathing. I heard him scream, a strangled howl, as he tried to get that precious oxygen into his lungs.

There's no way he's going to get up, I thought. But then

somehow he hauled himself to his feet – 'Wow!' I jumped on him again. He was already hurt and another couple of good shots would finish him off. But then the bell went – maybe there was someone looking down on him too.

That really was the problem. While I was all over Maidana in those early rounds, my speed and movement at its absolute best, he just carried on. He didn't look massively threatening but while he was still out there swinging there was always the chance he might land that one big blow. Thing is, you don't carry stats like Maidana's – at that point he'd lost just once, on a split decision, in thirty professional fights – unless there's something in it, and a minute into the tenth round he showed me just what his reputation had been built on. He caught me with a right-hander that felt like a collision with a concrete wall – just the sort of punch that, according to the 'experts', was guaranteed to have me on the floor with my tongue hanging out.

Surviving that round is one of *the* great achievements of my career. I knew that if I could just make it to the bell I had a chance. It's hard sometimes to describe how it feels to be in a real battle – I mean a *real* battle – but try to imagine what it's like to be hanging on for two minutes against an onslaught of that kind from a man like Maidana. Every time you try to get a second to recover, he's there in your vision, peering into your eyes, watching you like a hawk for any sign of weakening, the next attack imminent.

One way or another I survived the last two rounds. Maidana knew he was miles behind on points so he was looking desperately for that big knockout blow. I just about had it left in me to avoid his flailing fists. The decision in my favour was unanimous. It was an incredible win. One that gave me global respect in boxing. I had proved all those negative voices wrong. My chin – and I – had survived the biggest of tests. Anyone who wants to put it out there that I didn't have guts, try looking that particular bit of footage up on YouTube.

Truth is I have to watch that fight back myself to understand what happened. I don't actually remember any of it. I got hit that hard that it beat the memory out of me. I have a few five-second mental clips of being in the ambulance after the fight, going to the hospital for a check-up, coming back to my hotel room, and that's about it. It's not just the fight, for that whole day I don't remember nothing. No two ways about it, that fight took a few brain cells away.

For every thousand fights in boxing, there is one like this. It went down as an instant classic. Referee on the night, Joe Cortez, who'd been in the middle for fights featuring all-time greats like Roberto Duran and Mike Tyson, paid me a massive compliment when he put it in the top twenty fights he'd officiated. 'Blood, sweat and tears,' he said. 'That fight had it all.' He even compared my speed and punching power to Tyson's.

That was an amazing thing to hear, and yet nothing compared to what happened next. The Boxing Writers Association of America actually named it their Fight of the Year. That's quite something when you think about it. I mean, how many fights are there in a year? I'm so honoured to have been in that position where my fight was held up above all others. That will stay with me for the rest of my life – maybe my memory of those twelve rounds will come back one day too!

I still get messages from people saying they've just sat through that Maidana fight. The highlights pop up on American TV time and time again, and every time they do I get a reaction. But my fights often were the best fights. That sounds big-headed but I genuinely believe it to be true. People tune in to boxing because they want to see a spectacle, and I'm glad to say that, more often than not, I gave it to them. I'm also honest enough to say that sometimes that spectacle was me giving my best but still getting beat. That was the fate Freddie feared for me against Maidana. I'm glad Golden Boy saw it in more positive terms because that, more than any other, was the fight that made me. It gave me a massive profile in America.

The more I thought about it, the more I came to believe that everything about that night in Vegas was meant to happen. Me putting Maidana down and then him coming back and nearly taking my head off. It was a war, and genuinely I believe it was made that way by God. This was the fight that was going to show me to the world. God made that happen.

. . .

Afterwards, I hoped the 'glass chin' business would be well and truly dead in the water. I'd 100 per cent proven myself able to go in the ring with a guy known for leathering people. The way I saw it, if I could come through a test like that, I was never again going to be called out for supposedly being vulnerable to a big punch. Believe me, as a boxer, even when people say those words as a joke, which friends would occasionally, it affects you. I took it personally. It pissed me off that even after the wars I'd had, not to mention the entertainment I'd given, people would still say it to me. I'd think about it – 'I'm putting my life on the line to entertain people, and that's all you can think to say about it?' It was such a big insult. Same as if someone kept telling Lewis Hamilton he couldn't take a corner, or Ronaldo that he couldn't kick a ball. It would piss anyone off after a while.

For me, that endless chatter about my chin was jealously. Full stop. When people envy your ability, they find a way to put you down. It makes them feel better. Anytime anyone said it, honestly I thought it was pathetic. And I always had the ultimate reply – 'You think you can do better? Try putting yourself in the ring.'

It's the same with any kind of dissing in boxing. There's a complete lack of understanding of what it is to fight. I've heard people slag me off and actually said to them: 'Look, do you actually realise the hard work and sacrifice that goes into boxing? Do you understand the amount of training, the time away from our families, that we have to do to be at the top of our sport?' What used to upset me most of all was when another fighter said it. I'd look at their words and think, *You know how hard we train, the life we lead*. I'd see it as a total betrayal. I hate talking shit about anyone, but especially fighters, because I'm a fighter myself.

Boxers do get envious when others are more popular. I'm lucky enough to have always had a big following behind me, right back to the start at the Olympics and when I was getting mega viewing figures on ITV. Some fighters don't like that. They keep asking: 'Why not me?' Why not you? I'll tell you why not you. Because you didn't put in the hard work, or there's something about you that puts people off. The only reason I got a lot of adulation from the Olympics was because I put in the hard yards to get there in the first place. At the same time I always tried to be myself. People liked that – my popularity stemmed from there.

It's not just other boxers of course. In the twenty-first century, voices are everywhere. Somebody said to me the other day that for every idiot on social media who says something bad about me, there's another thousand who respect what I've done. Trouble is it's easier to focus on the negative one. Sometimes I'd have a pop back at someone having a go but it never helped. It just showed that I'd let them get to me. Stupid I know, but it can really affect your mood. In fact, that one person can mess it up for thousands of others.

There have been times when I've been due to appear at an event only to see something bad on social media and thought *You know what? I don't want to do it. I don't want to go out.* That's how bad these things are. They can get inside your head. That's why I'd urge any young fighter to get the mental training I never had.

People think we're untouchable, nothing will bother us, but inside we're normal people. We have soft hearts. I myself am actually a very soft personality, the type of guy who cares about people, can't say no. I'm a very innocent person, which is why at times, as we'll see, I've been walked over, ripped off, used and abused. I've been bullied – not physically, but verbally. People have stuck it on me and yes, it's hurt my feelings. When you have so much love from your sport, everything feels great. But then inevitably the negativity comes. Maybe people decide they just don't like you any more. Or maybe they no longer want to know you because you're not the big success story you once were. Mentally, that unexpected downer can destroy a fighter. When it comes, they need to be ready.

I genuinely believe that mental health training should be mandatory for boxers both during and after their careers, otherwise there will be a time when they feel lost, lonely and overwhelmed. I saw it when I visited the Boxing Hall of Fame in New York. Leon Spinks, an absolute icon of the sport, who became undisputed heavyweight champion of the world in 1978 after beating Muhammad Ali, was there, literally asking passers-by for a dollar. He'd gone from earning $13 million a fight to $5 an hour as a cleaner.

There are so many fighters who've lost everything. There are sharks out there, and a boxer with a few quid is their natural prey. Boxing has never had a support system for ex-fighters. They don't talk to anyone about mental health during their careers and they don't talk to anyone afterwards. The end result is that a lot of fighters have serious mental health issues in later life. They end up losing all their money because they've got no one to advise them. They end up drinking and gambling and often on their own because their relationships collapse. Think about it, you've been on that whole merry-go-round for years and then it stops. It doesn't slow down gradually. It's not like football where you might carry on down the leagues for a few seasons. It stops – dead. You're yesterday's news. Gone. That's a lonely place. I'm not joking when I say I know boxers who've harmed themselves.

There should always be someone there to talk to but quite often there isn't. A lot of fighters come from chaotic backgrounds. I'm lucky to have a strong family, but even I've fallen out with them down the years. Imagine what it's like if there was no proper family there in the first place. OK, that's where counsellors come in, but while that option might be available as part of a football club, boxing is an individual sport. At that point it's another expense, on what might be a tight budget. It's a non-starter.

For me, it's time boxing organised itself properly and funded an organisation, like the Professional Footballers' Association, which protects footballers and supports their rights and well-being. Boxing doesn't have an equivalent. I've talked about this a lot down the years, but nothing ever changes. Mad really. It's not like this is a hidden problem. Mike Tyson once told me he'd bought ten brand new

Bentleys and deliberately crashed them round Brooklyn or got bored and just dumped them at the side of the road. He wasn't telling me that as an example of his wild celebrity lifestyle, or to show off about the crazy amount of money he had. He was telling me to show how fucked up his head was.

Honestly, I think every boxer has a mental health issue at some point or another. Like I say, boxing is a sport where everyone is either with you or against you. When you're winning everyone wants a piece of you. When you're losing you're on your own – and you have to live with everyone saying how shit you are, how you can't fight, how, in my case, you've got a jaw that can't take a punch. I mean, I was a successful fighter, with a lot of support, and I still got a lot of criticism. You've got to have a very thick skin for it not to leave a mark. Even now, I have people come up to me and say: 'I never really liked you much when you were a boxer but you're actually an all right bloke.' I don't know what I'm supposed to say to that! I was the same person then as I am now. Does not knowing someone mean you should go round saying they're this and they're that?

I'll be honest, there's a big part of me that doesn't like talking about mental health because I don't want people thinking I'm making excuses, that I'm a wimp, or that I'm a softie. Being in boxing, I've always felt I have to be tough. There aren't many fighters out there willing to show any other side to themselves and I was no different. It's a character you have to maintain at all times. Otherwise how does it look? You're in a sport where you quite literally have to fight for everything you get. It becomes impossible to let that guard drop because people will immediately judge and mock you for it.

Maybe I should have spoken to someone about this when I was younger. I did actually once use a sports psychologist but my view at the time was I didn't feel there were any great benefits. I thought I knew all there was to know about me from a sports point of view. I could motivate myself to fight and switch off afterwards. And I knew God was watching over me, caring for me, at all times. But I'm sure there was a lot more that could have been discussed. I'll admit it – I'm scared to talk about mental health, but I know as well that if we don't then the next thing that happens is someone kills themselves. And yet so often our inner feelings are treated as a joke.

. . .

For now, after Maidana, I could put any negative voices out of my head. I'd succeeded in defending my WBA light-welterweight crown on three occasions. For the majority of the time I felt on top of the world, because that's exactly where I was. Sometimes it's not only your results that show you where you are in life. I attended a dinner only to be approached by a girl with my 'AK' logo tattooed on her wrist. Unusual, but not that unusual. What surprised me was when she then asked me to sign the skin below so she could have that inked in as well. I was happy to fulfil her request. I felt pretty much unbeatable at that stage so couldn't see her too quickly getting fed up of having a constant reminder of me on her wrist. I wonder how she feels now!

One person unlikely to join my fan on her tattoo journey was the promoter Barry Hearn. My next defence was against one of Barry's fighters, the Northern Irishman Paul McCloskey, back in Manchester. The fight was stopped in the sixth round after a clash of heads caused a cut over McCloskey's eye. I was ahead at the time and so was declared the winner. Let's just say Barry wasn't massively happy. I heard a commotion and turned round to see he'd climbed into the ring and was busy telling the referee: 'You're a fucking disgrace.' I got the idea he thought the fight should have been allowed to go on. I suppose it could have done but the result wouldn't have been any different. I'd have had McCloskey on the floor soon enough. I thought the fuss was crazy. The fight was over, done and dusted. Move on, Barry – nothing to see here.

Fights were coming thick and fast and just a few

months later I had the chance to unite the WBA and IBF light-welterweight titles by taking on the American, Zab Judah, back at Mandalay Bay. Judah, a great fighter in his day, was now nearing the end of his career. He couldn't match my sheer speed in the punch and around the ring and the inevitable knockout came in round five. The win meant I was a double world champion. It also meant I had scored eight straight victories, more often than not against testing opponents. The ghost of Breidis Prescott had been well and truly banished. The Judah fight was another where I'd been caught with a hook. It had barely registered. Judah, on the other hand, was heard telling someone at the post-fight press conference: 'I had no idea he could hit that hard.' He was right – I felt stronger, more muscular, than ever. Not only that but I was competing on a level playing field in and around the toughest weight divisions in the world. I was absolutely in my pomp – proper King Khan.

Inevitably, talk turned to a question, one that would follow me for the rest of my career. Actually, it still does even though I'm now retired – 'What about Floyd Mayweather?'

There are boxers and there are legends. When it comes to Floyd Mayweather, he's definitely in the second category. He was repeatedly voted the best pound-for-pound boxer in the world and claimed fifteen major titles across five weight classes. At one point he won twenty-six consecutive world title fights and would end with a 50–0 win–loss record. Many believe him to be the best of all time. When you put it like that, he probably deserves a category all of his own.

I knew I was on Mayweather's radar. He'd said in interviews he'd like to fight me in the UK and had even stated his preferred venue of Wembley – 'I'll keep my fingers crossed,' he said, 'and hope for the best.' Thing is, keeping your fingers crossed doesn't actually make these things happen. I wanted that fight at that time as much as he said he did, but I was just one of several contenders trying to get his name in the diary. To meet Mayweather the planets really did have to align – but after I'd beaten Judah the stars looked finally to have turned my way. This time there was real progress on behind-the-scenes talks and a deal was put on the table. When I signed my side of the contract I was so excited. I knew I was at the peak of my career. I was on fire. Genuinely, I felt *I'm gonna destroy this guy.*

And then, just at the point when it looked like the fight was nailed on to happen, the planets started to slip away again. Mayweather started trying to put me off my game. First of all he started arguing over money. I don't know why. To fight him at that point of my career I'd have agreed to anything – and I told him as much.

When that didn't work, he then started pointing to an

interview I'd done where I'd mentioned we were close to making the fight happen and that I'd signed my side of the contract. It was then that he went proper crazy. Apparently, in Mayweather's eyes, it's a crime for anyone to announce, or even mention, a fight before him. As far as he was concerned, that was it – the deal was off. And that, in a nutshell, is why I never fought Floyd Mayweather. Bit childish really. The words 'toys', 'pram' and 'throw' spring to mind. You can reason with most things in life, ego isn't one of them – although in all honesty I 100 per cent think he was just using the announcement timing as an excuse. You can tell when someone is running away from a fight and that's exactly what Mayweather was doing. I was flying at that point, the fastest fighter out there, while he was becoming slower and more predictable. To fight me at that stage would have been a massive test, a real risk to his treasured unbeaten record. He couldn't beat me on reach, he couldn't beat me on speed, and his ability to land a solid series of punches had waned. I didn't need to make it a war to beat him. I could take my time – hit and move – turn it into a tactical encounter and get a victory on points. People might doubt whether a man like Mayweather would ever run from a fight but look at who he went on to fight twice in a year – Marcos Maidana, who I'd already beaten. I genuinely believe he knew I had his number.

Mayweather might have slipped from my grasp but his antics didn't change how I felt about myself at that time. People ask what it feels like to be right at the top, the one who's gone from just another challenger to the person everybody wants to beat; to get in the ring and be flying. The answer is easy. Powerful. Very powerful. At that point, for once in your career, you feel in total control. You are doing something you've worked hard towards, that you love, and are having a great time showing the world how good you are at it. You open the newspaper and see your name being put up there against the biggest names in the sport, like Manny and Mayweather. When you start out as a kid, that is exactly what you want to achieve. And, like I say, I'd actually achieved twice. This was my second mountain. Athens had been my first. By allowing me to win silver in Greece, God had given me the confidence to achieve everything else I was now doing in the sport. That's important, because in boxing the pressure is always on. There's a lot of fighters in this world who deliver one or two good fights but then just can't maintain that standard. They can't keep performing at a high level all the time. I wasn't like them. I was always going to stick at it. In the end, it's that determination that delivers the real 'Wow!' moments in a career, like when you look out from the ring and see that the biggest of big names – Mike Tyson, Lennox

Lewis – have come to see you fight. You win titles, but you also win respect.

That respect, that status, was no better exemplified than when, on the tenth anniversary of the 9/11 attacks, US Secretary of State Hillary Clinton invited me to attend a White House dinner she was hosting for Muslim athletes. I would be the only non-American there. For me the invite was a 'hair on the back of the neck' moment – a point where I really saw the global unifying significance of sport. I never thought of anything I did in terms of a phrase like 'multi-culturalism'. I just wanted people to see they had more in common than what divides them. I just wanted them to get on.

Being at the White House made me think about how 9/11 had affected me. After the attacks I had been looked on with suspicion. Trying to get into the US as someone with Pakistani heritage was especially difficult. Anyone like me was seen not as an individual but as either a potential terrorist or a terrorist sympathiser. The customs guys would flick through my passport, see that I'd been to Saudi Arabia – unsurprising since it's an important place of pilgrimage – and Pakistan and react like public enemy number one had turned up. They'd ask if I'd ever been to Iraq and when I'd last fired a weapon. I'd point out that I was a boxer who'd come over for a scheduled fight. It wasn't exactly hard to find out if that was true – the event would be right there on the internet. But still the ridiculous questions would carry on.

I'd be taken out the queue and moved to a holding room while various enquiries were made. Three hours later they'd realise I was just some boxer from England and let me go. I have to say being invited to Hillary's dinner improved things a lot on that front, especially since it came up in conversation. I don't know what she did, but things were a lot better from then on.

After the dinner I was pleased to be able to return the invite to Hillary – my next fight was scheduled for Washington. If she had a night off she could come along. As it turned out, she'd have made a much better referee than the one who was actually in the ring.

That same year, 2011, I was nominated for BBC Sports Personality of the Year, alongside big-hitters like golfer Rory McIlroy and tennis star Andy Murray. I was a bit of an outsider with the bookies and the cyclist Mark Cavendish won on the night. Boxing and pro cycling are worlds apart, although me and Mark would later have something neither of us wanted in common when, within the space of six months, we were both robbed of watches in front of our partners and under the threat of our lives.

On a brighter note, I had won Sports Personality of the Year at the British Asian Sports Awards, and while I might not have won BBC Sports Personality it did feel like pretty much everything else in my life was falling into place. A few months earlier, through a bunch of friends, I'd met a girl at a party in New York. Her name was Faryal Makhdoom, a nineteen-year-old student at Rutgers University School of Arts and Sciences in New Jersey. Right away something clicked in me. I didn't see Faryal as just another girl. She was special and even then I couldn't help thinking she was someone I'd love to marry. I think I might even have mentioned she was marriage material because later she said she thought I was a 'total bullshitter'!

I can see why she'd have thought like that – I was five years older than her after all. But even then she seemed very grown up. She was certainly more sensible than me. She was studying political science and journalism. I fought for a living. I'm puzzled to this day what she saw in a boxer! Maybe she couldn't understand what I was telling her! In those early days, it would take her a while to translate my accent. More often than not whenever I said anything she'd just look at me and nod. Thankfully, we did have a common link – our Pakistani heritage.

I fell for Faryal from the start – they say opposites attract after all – and was keen to invite her over to England. I say 'keen', actually I pretty much begged her to see me. Fortunately, she agreed. I thought I'd save the bright lights of Bolton for later – there's only so much a girl can take – and so we met in London.

I was eager to make a good impression and so was delighted when a friend lent me a Rolls-Royce. What better way to take Faryal out to dinner? I arrived at her hotel and couldn't help thinking this must look pretty cool, this must be impressing her. We were driving through the British capital, past all the big famous landmarks, in the most renowned of grand English cars. I was just thinking how pleased I was with myself to have pulled this off when I saw the blue lights of a police car in the rear-view mirror.

It was the classic knock on the window – 'Excuse me, sir. Is this your vehicle?'

I couldn't help thinking how this wasn't in the script for the evening I'd spent the last few days so carefully planning in my head.

'Er, no. It belongs to a friend.'

'Hmm. OK.' He didn't sound convinced. 'Only we've put the registration through the computer and the car is showing up as uninsured.'

Next thing we knew, me and my dream date were standing on the pavement wondering if instead of a top-class meal at a fancy restaurant we might end up with a cup of cold tea in the cells. I could just imagine how that would go down with the prospective in-laws. The first time we were out on our own and this happened! I mean, what do you say? 'Oh, sorry for causing your daughter to spend half the night at the police station. It won't happen again, honest.'

Luckily the owner was able to find the relevant paperwork and we were allowed on our way, but I was still worried. Instead of looking cool, suave and sophisticated, the whole thing now had an air of *this is what happens when you go out on a date with a famous boxer*. As first dates go, it was the worst nightmare.

I was able to make amends soon after by heading over to New York to make a better impression. Three months later, my marriage prediction came true – we were formally engaged. The ceremony happened at Bolton's Reebok Stadium where I presented Faryal with a £100,000 platinum engagement ring. Bolton Wanderers players Kevin Davies and Jussi Jääskeläinen watched on as well as Manchester United legends Wayne Rooney and Rio Ferdinand.

Bolton might not seem the obvious place for us to celebrate an engagement, especially when one half of the couple is from New York, but if Faryal was going to get to know me properly then she'd also have to get to know the place that made me. And that was Bolton, Greater Manchester, England. Some people said it must have been a bit of a culture shock for her, among them Jonathan

Ross. When I went on his chat show he couldn't resist comparing the magnificent architecture of Manhattan to Bolton bus station. Obviously, Bolton isn't New York. We have Primark not Macy's. But Faryal is an intelligent woman. She is educated and understands that places are about more than bricks and mortar. It says everything about her that instead of pushing my background away she embraced it. One thing you have to understand about Faryal is that she is imaginative and ambitious. She didn't see a move to England as a negative. She saw it as an opportunity to build her own profile as a successful businesswoman.

• • •

Maybe with so much going on outside boxing it's no surprise that the actual trophies of my success – the belts – ended up a little neglected. But then again that's what happens. It's weird, all that time, effort, blood, sweat and tears that goes into winning a belt and then when finally you get your hands on one you haven't the faintest idea what to do with it. You keep it out for a few weeks so people can see it, touch it, have a photo, and then inevitably it ends up shoved under the bed in a box.

For many years I did that. Some of it was being brought up to be humble, not to be a show-off, but a lot of it was like, *What the hell am I actually meant to do with this?* It makes me laugh. I used to have video game evenings with my mates and whoever won would take a belt home for the night. I'm not sure that's quite what these global boxing organisations have in mind when they're dishing out these things.

One of the best things Faryal has ever done for me is install a big glass frame for all my belts. I walk in now, physically see them, and it really stops me in my tracks and makes me think about what I achieved at the peak of my career. These days I like to see them, to remember the different stories they tell – to show people and be proud.

When you win anything, never keep it under the bed! It's a reminder of the good times. Believe me, they never last for ever.

COACHING SESSION 6

Successful people will often drown out negative noise by surrounding themselves with 'yes' people. You know the sort – basically they're there to blow smoke up someone's arse and tell them everything about them is magnificent. I never had that. Even at my most successful, I always had people around me to keep my feet on the ground.

Sport, especially boxing, can be brutal from that point of view, but honesty is vital to progression. I might have disagreed with those who kept banging on about my 'glass chin' but I never stopped listening to voices I respected. If they had criticisms to make, or identified lessons to be learned, I listened. If I hadn't done that, I'd have stood still. Worse, if I'd surrounded myself with 'yes' people I'd have gone backwards. Find good people, let them be open and honest, and you will get a long way in life.

ROUND SEVEN

Something was wrong. You can't keep hitting someone that hard and they just carry on coming back at you. It's impossible. It defies the limits of physical strength.

Lamont Peterson had an energy that just wasn't right. It was like boxing someone who was beyond human. In pro cycling they describe people like this as 'out of this world'. It's a way of saying something without actually saying it – that someone's on drugs.

Perhaps I shouldn't have been surprised. Everything else felt weighted against me for this title defence – the referee, the venue. Why should my opponent be any different?

Peterson was a solid fighter. He'd come from a tough start in life, abandoned by his parents and living on the streets before finding a saviour in boxing. He'd beaten a few decent names but I was confident not just of beating him but beating him convincingly. Initially our fight was scheduled for Vegas but in the end it was switched to Washington, DC, Peterson's home city, and one that hadn't staged a top-flight title challenge for almost twenty years. I was about to find out why that might be.

I'd heard it said a few times in my career – never fight in Washington, DC, it's a 'home' city, meaning there were suspicions of bouts being weighted in the home fighter's favour. I ignored the gossip but fighting Peterson on his own turf was always going to be tricky. One of them where you feel you're two rounds behind on the scorecards before you've even got in the ring.

On the other hand, I'd really liked the city when I'd been there for the Hillary Clinton dinner and as Freddie was quick to remind me, 'the ring is the same size wherever you are'. It was also an opportunity to build an audience outside the traditional boxing centres of Vegas and New York. Yes, the vast majority of the sell-out 9,000 crowd at the Walter E. Washington Convention Center would be screaming for Peterson, but it would be nothing I couldn't handle.

And that's exactly how things were panning out. I put Peterson on his backside twice in the first round. Normally you'd go on to dominate from that kind of position but no matter how hard and how often I hit him it made no difference. He just kept coming and coming. That's not right. Hit someone hard and it saps their energy. It's like puncturing a tyre. Bit by bit the air comes out until there's nothing left. With Peterson, the tyre pressure never changed. No matter what I did, it didn't affect him. In fact, if anything he seemed to be getting stronger and stronger. OK, he'd got a big crowd behind him, but there's only so much difference that can make. It doesn't change the basic laws of fighting – getting hit hard makes you lose strength. I was too in-the-moment to be suspicious. Only afterwards did I really start to think.

With Lamont being unbreakable, the fight went the distance. Which is when something else weird happened. As the scorecards were being verified, a mysterious man in a black hat appeared. He leaned over the fight supervisor's shoulder and could clearly be seen speaking to him. It's written in stone that no one is allowed near the officials when the cards are being marked or checked but this man was clearly right in the thick of it.

The 'man in the hat' became a source of great puzzlement to all and sundry until he was eventually revealed as Mustafa Ameen, who was connected to the IBF but still shouldn't have been within a million miles of the scorecards. His explanation was he was pointing out a basic adding-up mistake. This apparently isn't a problem – feel free to nip down to the official's table and poke your oar in next time you're at a fight.

I'd already felt the referee Joe Cooper was singling me out after docking me two, as it turned out vital, points for pushing. It was a crazy decision. Peterson had kept using his head, coming in low, like a headbutt, and when that happens you have no choice. Nothing happened in that fight that didn't happen in a thousand others – but suddenly here it was a problem?

With first the ref, who had also only registered one of my two first-round knockdowns, and now the man in the hat, it really did fuel my paranoia that the fight was going to be judged on more than purely boxing. I'm not big on conspiracy theories but, mad as it might sound, it really did seem like the cards were stacked to make sure I was never going to win. And that's exactly what happened. The judges scored the fight 113–112, 113–112, 110–115 in favour of the local hero, the docked points proving the difference on the two cards in Peterson's favour, this despite my camp being told unofficially that the fight had gone my way by a split decision. To add to the farce, the MC even read out the scores wrong and announced Peterson had won by a majority rather than a split decision. The whole thing had turned into one very bad joke.

My first reaction when I'd heard the fight was going to be in Washington was *Oh shit!* – given the rumours I'd heard. I felt like I'd been one man against a tag team – Peterson, the referee, the judges and, possibly, the man in the hat. I became convinced that you could have stuck peak Mike Tyson in that ring, he could have knocked Peterson through the ropes after thirty seconds, and he still wouldn't have won. In boxing they talk about 'home cooking'. If that's what this was, I'll be straight – I didn't like the taste.

To say I was gutted would be an understatement. It's

not just the losing when you know you've won, it's what it can mean further down the line. Promoters aren't interested in the fine details, they just see the word 'loss'. I'd come out of the ring unscathed and yet more damaged than I'd ever been.

I felt robbed, but at the same time I didn't allow myself to get angry. Instead of me standing there ranting and looking like a sore loser I allowed what had happened to speak for itself. Which it did – anyone who saw that fight was saying they couldn't believe what had just happened. It was them saying I was robbed, that I never lost the fight, that the result had no credibility, and this was why big fights never happened in DC. Put simply, it was a fight that was giving boxing a bad name. In the end, I appealed the decision but it never got fully investigated because – surprise, surprise – Lamont tested positive for performance-enhancing drugs. He had a testosterone pellet embedded in his hip.

You'd think that would mean the decision would be overruled and I'd get my belts back. But this is boxing – nothing is ever quite that simple. Initially, before the drugs test results, there was talk of a rematch, something I favoured – a quick way to show everyone how much of a superior boxer I was to Peterson and how the original result had been a scandal. I was actually working towards that rematch when the chance of redemption was scuppered by the testosterone revelation. Instead, the WBA did reinstate my belt. The IBF, however, ruled that while Peterson had been found to have used testosterone it wasn't enough to have affected his performance.

I don't know what channel they were watching on TV that night, but it obviously wasn't the fight. There was only one reason Peterson fought the way he did. No one had ever seen him fight like that before. For me, that was a bad ruling. Peterson was out of control. That didn't just mean he could have inflicted damage, lasting damage, on me, he could have inflicted it on himself. We were belting the hell out of each other for twelve rounds. Really hitting hard. I'm sure in any other circumstances I'd have won on a knockout. But he never stepped back, never recoiled from a hit. Even when I had him on the floor in the first round he was straight back up. If he didn't feel the pain how could he know what was happening to himself? It's like a car engine screaming at maximum revs for an hour. It'll do it, but there's a price to pay for that kind of abuse.

In making that decision, the IBF basically told boxers it was all right to be a cheat. I had a lot of hard fights. Nothing was ever like that one – but those drugs weren't performance enhancing? Boxing had a problem and it didn't want to admit it. That's the problem with the professional boxing world. It makes its own rules and its decisions can be baffling. Boxing, a sport about stamina and strength, is ripe for drug abuse. There is testing but you can imagine there always have been, and always will be, people doing it. In my case that means that a fight which, by anybody's standards, I clearly won, even against an opponent who had added another layer of armour by cheating, is in the records as a loss. It also means, as we shall see later, that the presence of banned drugs in and around boxing can mean an innocent fighter being tarred with the same brush.

At least I had a nice distraction, and a reminder of better times, when, ahead of London 2012, I was asked to be part of the Olympic torch relay, carrying it into Bolton where a cauldron was lit in Queen's Park. Around 10,000 people lined the streets of the town, which was incredible really, especially since by now I had gone on to find a life away from Bolton. It was a humbling experience and one which did a lot to remind me who I was and where I came from. I couldn't help but also remember how I'd sat in front of the TV and watched Muhammad Ali light the flame, hand shaking from his Parkinson's disease, at the Atlanta Olympics in 1996. The link between then and now – I'm not sure if a boxer had carried the torch since – made it an incredibly emotional occasion.

If I was again to taste the kind of acclaim that came my way during the Athens Games, I needed a fight that would rebuild a reputation tarnished by matters out of my control. A fight definitely not staged in Washington! Danny Garcia, a young Philadelphian fighter with a decent pedigree, seemed to fit the bill. The fight was arranged for Las Vegas. Everything was good. It felt like I'd found a route that would put me back on course without too much damage being caused. I'd beat Garcia and in the process reinforce the fact that Peterson was a rogue fight. What I was actually heading towards was the lowest point of my fighting career and one that again I could and should have totally avoided.

• • •

This time my downfall started in a place where it never should – in the pre-fight press conference. These are places for a bit of nonsense, a bit of to and fro bullshit to add spice to a fight, provide a couple of easy headlines and get the box office ticking. It wasn't Danny but his trainer dad Angel who lit the blue touch paper. He'd already said that I was overrated and Peterson had 'whupped' me 'like an octopus'. But that didn't bother me. What got me spewing was when he said my DNA was 'fucked up' and that he'd never seen 'a Pakistani who can fight'. Puerto Rican by birth, Angel stated: 'This is Latino blood, a nation – we are going to show the world who's the boss.'

I thought of my own dad and the quiet dignity with which he held himself around these important pre-fight moments, and now here was Angel Garcia dissing our heritage. I wasn't impressed. In all honesty it was all I could do not to put his lights out there and then. But I let him know I was going to knock his son flat out instead. Angel later denied being a racist. He must just have been doing a good impression of one.

It didn't really matter whether Angel meant it or not, he'd done his job. He'd got under my skin. The point of doing that to anyone is to divert them from their game plan. It happens in all sports. Footballers say stuff to each other on the pitch. Darts players slow their play down to irritate an opponent. Cricketers sledge. It's what goes on, and that's what happened here. Angel Garcia got me so wound up that instead of sticking to a plan I went in that ring to hurt someone. A few years later it would never have worked but I was still only twenty-five at that point, immature enough for someone to get to me.

Sounds odd for a sport that's so combative, where the script, the trash talk, is all about wanting to rip the other guy's head off, but I've never used hate as a driving factor. I've heard about it happening in other sports – in football and rugby for example, where they'll build a team hatred for the opposition – but it's never been a thing for me. Probably a good job, because the one time I was made to feel hate, and took it into the ring, it backfired completely.

Hate is an emotion that can make you lose control and do something stupid. I shouldn't have been carrying it around with me. The place to actually lay into opponents is the ring. Why waste time and energy doing the same in your mind? That doesn't mean I'm going to tell an opponent before a fight that I think he's a great fighter, someone I really respect. Before the fight I'll stir things up to make people feel like, *Wow! I really want to watch this fight*, and get everyone talking about it. But afterwards I'll be the first one to go for a coffee with the guy, talk properly to him. At that point we've had our business transaction. Let's move on. I don't hate no one. I don't want to be seen like that. I think people like me because there's so many different sides to my personality. I can be serious when I need to be and have a laugh a lot of the time too. I'm glad I've done a lot of TV shows down the years because that's where people get to see me as a fully defined person, a normal guy.

If Breidis Prescott was a low point then it was nothing compared to Danny Garcia. This was a fight with so much on the line, not just the unification of the World Boxing Council (WBC) and WBA titles but, after Peterson, the repair of my career. Prescott could, to some degree at least, be put down to early years naivety. Garcia? That was just a really bad personal error.

I was well ahead, cruising really, when in the third round I let my concentration slip, going for big shots instead of just steadily wearing Garcia into the ground. It was then that Garcia caught me with a massive left hook. I survived the thirty seconds to the bell but the steam had gone from me and he finished the job off as I vainly tried to attack in round four. That's what happens in boxing when you take your eye off the ball. Any half-decent opponent will see it straight away, pounce, and have you on the floor. It's a sport that doesn't do second chances.

I was devastated. To get beat is one thing. To get beat and it be your own fault is entirely another. All I had to do was carry on what I was doing and the fight was in the bag. In no way, shape or form was I troubled. The Garcia fight was a ladder with no sign of a snake. I was 1/7 on with the bookies. It was a chance to reaffirm to the entire boxing world that I was at my peak – bring on the big boys! Instead I'd lost my place in the pecking order and reignited that whole tiresome nonsense – 'Amir Khan? He's got a glass chin.' Even now, I don't think I ever quite recovered my reputation after Garcia. It was too big a blow at precisely the wrong time.

Post-fight parties are a thing in Vegas. Mine was at the LAX nightclub at the Luxor. Turning up as the loser wasn't in the plan, but well, as I made my way through crowds of revellers to the VIP area and the DJ announced: 'Amir Khan is in the building!' – which I could maybe have done without – I thought it might at least take my mind off what had just happened. I knew I wouldn't be able to sleep if I went back to the hotel anyway. It was a way of forgetting, switching off.

As it turned out that party was one of my last glimpses of the big showbiz lifestyle. I was beginning to wonder if certain things had begun to affect my performance as a boxer – and being around celebrities, living that A-list lifestyle, was one of them. No two ways about it, it had definitely turned my head. Even at the gym it affected me. Having big stars coming to see me train was great and everything but too often it turned practice into performance. Instead of targeting what I should have been doing, I was showing them what I could do. You want to emphasise that you're special – like they are. Just doing a normal sparring session, or maybe even someone showing you up a little bit, doesn't really fit in with a 'big-time' reputation.

It's odd how you can get caught up in something like that. I loved meeting all these amazing people but, at the same time, friends come and go so quickly in LA that you can never be sure what the word actually means. I suppose really we come back to that old thing of people only wanting to know you so long as you're winning. And that only happens if you concentrate on how they got to know you in the first place – your skill at boxing. Let that go and you're nowhere.

I recalled how in the run-up to the Garcia fight I'd been to four parties. Jennifer Lopez had been at one of them. And then I thought about how I used to sacrifice a social life as a kid because I wanted to be a champion so much. I don't think Mick Jelley would have been too impressed with me attending four parties, Jennifer Lopez or no Jennifer Lopez. In fact, I'm pretty sure Mick Jelley wouldn't have recognised Jennifer Lopez if she'd passed him in Bolton high street!

There was another major reality check when I came back to the UK. Me and my brother Haroon had been out to a concert in Birmingham one Sunday night and then gone on to meet some friends at a shisha lounge. My own car had broken down on the way and we were in a courtesy car, a Range Rover. It was weird because during the evening someone said to us that there was a group of men following us around. I didn't really think anything of it – they could have been anyone – but in the shisha lounge I could just tell the vibe wasn't right. I didn't really feel comfortable and so suggested we drive somewhere else. We paid and left but just as I was going to unlock the car door some guys appeared. There's nothing unusual about that. Wherever I go, people end up asking for autographs or taking pictures. But then when I turned back to the car I realised someone was inside. At first I thought I'd got the wrong car – that I'd got confused because it was a courtesy car. But no, I looked again and it was definitely the right Range Rover.

'What are you doing in my car?'

'What are you going to do about it?'

He came round and punched me in the face. It wasn't the best punch I'd ever been on the end of – more of a weak jab. Whatever, it's never a good idea to punch a boxer, not only because they're skilled fighters, but because their automatic reaction is to punch you back – hard. Which I did. They'd definitely picked the wrong people to start on. By now Haroon was an accomplished boxer too and had a Commonwealth Games bronze medal for Pakistan to prove it. Neither of us were going to let people bully us in the street. As soon as the fighting started, that was it. Guys started running towards us with coshes and chains. We jumped in the car and drove off.

I've never lived my life behind a wall. I've always gone places where everyone goes because I like being around people and doing normal things. I suppose as someone in the public eye I should have thought more about the risks and been more careful. But I was reckless – a young, reckless boy. I just thought that the world was a nice place. I wasn't nervous. I wasn't scared. But I could have been in serious trouble many times. Even now I take things for granted. I'm too nice a person. I think it's never going to happen to me. But there are bad people in the world – and my luck very nearly did run out a few years later. Be one step ahead is the golden rule.

Maybe it was time to take a more measured approach. Certainly I knew that as a professional fighter I couldn't ever again be beaten so easily and openly. I needed to be better equipped to see off an onslaught. It was time for another big and bold decision. Freddie Roach and Los Angeles had been amazing for me. No doubt about it, going with Freddie had changed both my life and career. His coaching style had made me one of the most exciting fighters on the planet, and, like I say, from a popularity point of view it's not a bad thing to be vulnerable. It's just that I was starting to feel a little too vulnerable. It was time to shore up the defences.

. . .

Virgil Hunter was a trainer renowned for producing tough, uncompromising boxers who were hard to beat. After two ticks in the 'loss' column, I quite fancied a bit of his defensive sparkle landing on me. That meant a hike up the coast to Union City near San Francisco, a place so unlike LA you'd struggle to understand how it could be in the same country, let alone state. Its complete lack of stardust was perfect for me. What I needed was peace and quiet; time to consider my future and rebuild. I also needed Virgil, someone to reinstall a balance of attack and defence. I knew some people would have a pop at me for making the switch, as if I was blaming Freddie rather than myself for the defeat, but in boxing you never stop learning. I believed Virgil could make me a better all-round competitor. He could build that vital extra layer of protection.

From the off Virgil wasn't one to pussyfoot around. If he saw me doing something he wasn't happy with, in particular being too open, he'd be straight in there – 'What the hell are you doing?' That might seem a bit of an abrupt way to talk to someone who's been world champion but the best trainers don't care who you are. They just want you to get better, and if that means getting in your face a bit, so be it. In Virgil's case, he didn't want to train someone who looked good but lost. He wanted to rein me in a bit. That did in some ways go against my instinct but more important than that was to rescue my career. Virgil showed me I could win, still be my natural fast flamboyant self, but be more guarded against that single killer blow.

Our partnership got off to a good start with victory

over the American, Carlos Molina, in his own backyard of LA. I looked controlled and measured but beneath the surface there was a lot more going on. I was coming off the back of the biggest hiccup of my career. Lose three fights in a row and I could forget the American dream. Molina was the barrier at the crossroads. Get over it and hopefully I could carry on forwards to the big fights that I wanted to define my career. Mess up and I was on the slippery slope to being a bit-part player on an undercard in a dingy sports hall in Britain. In boxing, wrapped up in TV rights and promoters seeking the biggest commercial opportunities, you are soon forgotten.

I received a big morale boost from the UK fans who came over for the fight plus the support of Vinnie Jones in the audience. I've always had a great relationship with footballers and at the pre-fight press conference had worn a cap donated by Rio Ferdinand. Maybe footballers know what it's like to be written off; to be the golden boy one week and the butt of everybody's jibes the next. I had big respect for them. I'd go under the microscope twice a year. They had it fifty times a season.

With Molina dispatched, I made a return to England for what turned out to be a much tougher and full-on battle against Julio Díaz, a hard-hitting fighter in true Mexican style. In many ways, it was the perfect fight to show that what Virgil was instilling in me, that tougher defence, was working. Díaz actually had me down in the fourth round, although that was more to do with me losing my footing than anything, and never stopped looking for a repeat of the knockout blow that had worked so well for Garcia.

It was another classic Khan fight, a great spectacle of two fighters really going at it. The point is that, with a new defensive strategy, I was never really threatened and won by a unanimous decision. When I then took out the former WBA welterweight champion Luis Collazo at the MGM Grand in Las Vegas, making a mockery of his hands-down technique by putting him on the floor three times, and then totally overwhelmed Devon Alexander at the same venue – in a pair of shorts with a 24-carat gold thread waistband no less – I really felt like I'd earned my place back at the top table.

Talking of top tables, after the Díaz fight myself and Faryal celebrated our marriage. It was a small affair – not! First up we had the actual ceremony at New York's vast Waldorf Astoria hotel. Nothing was understated, including our colour co-ordinated costumes of red, silver and white. Faryal's dress was covered in the most incredible gems while I wore a traditional Pakistani tunic complete with crimson turban. I have to say we did look pretty good!

I was incredibly lucky to have found someone as

beautiful and caring as Faryal, someone willing to give up their own life in New York to share mine. I was only twenty-six but by then I felt I'd lived the lives of ten people and was more than ready to take on the responsibilities of a family man.

After the ceremony me and Faryal had a dance-off. Thankfully, it was more than just ourselves – I don't think I could have lived with the embarrassment. I joined up with friends for a Bollywood routine that I think just about justified what had felt like an entire training camp of choreography. I'm not sure it was worth the bother – Faryal and her bridesmaids wiped the floor with us. I was glad of a golden throne to sit on to recover. If energy levels dropped I could also have a slice of the six-foot wedding cake. I'd travelled a fair way from being that little kid in shorts nicking a slice off the teacher's desk.

If the bash in New York was extravagant then the one back in the UK at EventCity, a massive exhibition space in Manchester, wasn't exactly low-budget. More than a thousand guests attended, including Wayne Rooney, David Haye and Ricky Hatton, while me and Faryal flew in by helicopter from Bolton. This time the cake was fourteen feet tall – well, there were a lot more guests than in New York.

Those celebrations – they seemed to go on for ever – on both sides of the Atlantic are something I never want to forget. The love we had from everyone around us was amazing.

I got to thinking about creating an amazing wedding venue in Bolton itself. As you might have realised I have a habit of not doing things by halves, and this was no different. The idea was to create a wedding and banqueting hall, with all-glass frontage, and multiple other businesses including a cosmetics and beauty outlet for Faryal and a rooftop shisha bar for me! OK, it wasn't for everyone but I did quite fancy having my own shisha bar. There would also be restaurants and other places to hang out and all in all there'd be around 200 jobs created.

It all looked great on the drawing board. In reality it would turn out to be the biggest of never-ending headaches, one which not only drained me of millions of pounds but in some ways very nearly cost me my relationship with my family. There would be many times over the next few years when I wished I'd never clapped eyes on that patch of land. It felt like people were constantly dipping into my pocket but nothing ever got done. I was left staring at the same old half-finished 'masterpiece', the same old dismal building site, the same old overriding question – *when will this ever be finished?*

Fortunately, there was some seriously great news round the corner. Myself and Faryal hadn't been married a year when a beautiful baby girl, Lamaisah, came along, a landmark moment in anybody's life and one which made me think more about my own future than I had for a while. Now I had real responsibility – a child. How long did I want to carry on in the riskiest sport of them all? I was by no means thinking of retiring – I was only twenty-seven at the time – but I knew I didn't want to go on and on for ever like some boxers do. I wanted to enjoy family life, not tune into it occasionally from training camps.

That wider attitude to life, the altering of perspective that comes with responsibility, a realisation that the world far from revolves around yourself, also showed its face by me setting up the Amir Khan Foundation. I'd seen from an early age that I couldn't exist in a bubble outside of the world's problems. Even if I'd wanted to, some of them were way too close to home for that to happen – remember the Pakistani earthquake that had taken family members of people we knew? I wanted to set up an organisation that not only was ready to respond to disasters but would help struggling people and communities in the UK and across the world.

I'm pleased to say that in the years since, that's exactly what we've done, be it by sending aid to flood victims in Bangladesh or to help people suffering from food poverty in the UK and India. Again, this work has so much to do with my belief in God. I'm a spiritual person. God has helped me and instilled in me a belief in helping others. I look at the determination of those who have nothing, their willpower to create and survive, to find a way to put food on the table, and I realise that what we in sport call strength is nothing compared to that. I think how I've got everything I want and sometimes struggle for motivation. It's really humbling to see, right there in front of you, the true meaning of struggle.

I can definitely say the foundation has opened my eyes to those a lot less fortunate than myself. After Ukraine was invaded by Russia, for example, I went to Poland to meet refugees from the war and see first-hand its terrible impact on their lives. It meant such a lot that the foundation could actually help out on the ground. One of the things it could do in this instance was help to provide a fitness playground for a refugee home which housed those orphaned by the conflict. We could also deliver food, clothing and first aid training.

Perhaps the most distressing sight that ever faced me was the remains of a school in Peshawar in Pakistan where 141 people, mostly children, were massacred by the Taliban. I couldn't believe what I was hearing, how terrorists had gone from classroom to classroom killing innocent children. It was sick beyond belief. What kind of person does something like that?

As a new parent myself, I found it almost too much to bear. I wanted to go there for one reason – to help. It was no good me going there and collapsing at the horror of it all. Those poor families who had lost children were the ones who had truly suffered. As hard as it was I tried to detach myself emotionally. You need to be strong in a situation like that, to show your respect, and show that terrorism and violence will never win. I wanted to help rebuild the school, whether that be by creating publicity about an incident which, sadly, was one of many, and so soon forgotten in the West, or by auctioning those 24-carat Devon Alexander fight shorts for a five-figure sum.

Pakistan is a country I love and to see it being blown apart by extremists – for what? – was horrible. I hated the way these people were trying to tear a hole in this great land and its people. I hated the way the actions of these murderers were holding Pakistan back so much. If anything I said or did could make even the tiniest amount of difference to the battle against these disgusting people with their bombs and their guns then I was happy to go there again and again. There are some people who cannot be allowed to win.

COACHING SESSION 7

Standing up for yourself and what you believe in is important. We live in times when people are shouted down, both in real life and on social media. In the face of such hostility it's easy to turn away and stop talking about what's important to you. But then the bullies have won.

Be confident in being true to yourself and you will find your self-esteem is the winner. You will feel energised by engaging with your beliefs rather than stifling them. I know – because that's exactly what happened to me. There have been many occasions where I could have taken the easy option and turned away. But I never have and never will. If people don't like what I say, they don't have to listen. But I hope they will because my key message is one of peace and hope. Whatever your message is, never let anyone silence you or rein you in. Being able to speak is central to our well-being.

ROUND EIGHT

Daring to be great. You either do it or you don't. Personally I never wanted to waste my best boxing years going through the motions. And that's what I was at risk of doing while I waited, and waited, for another chance of the fight against Floyd Mayweather.

His last three fights had been against Saul 'Canelo' Alvarez, Marcos Maidana and Manny Pacquiao. His well of proven opposition was running dry. Down the years, as I'd chased the fight, Mayweather had told me to prove myself at 147 pounds. Having just convincingly beaten Luis Collazo and Devon Alexander at that weight, I felt I had sent out yet another message – 'OK, Floyd, here I am. I'm ready!' But again, while there were bits of chatter, nothing had got near to being confirmed. From that point of view, the defeat to Danny Garcia remained a visible bruise on my career, the one that could always be held against me, and brand me as not deserving a roll of the dice.

If ever I needed confirmation of that, it came when I went to watch a fight between Garcia and Robert Guerrero in Los Angeles. There, sat in front of me, was Mayweather. I don't know why he felt he had to do it, but he turned and faced me.

'Is this the guy that beat you?' he asked. He knew full well the answer to that question. He just wanted to wind me up.

I had a better question for him – 'Why won't you fight me?' – and he didn't like it. I knew why. There was no valid answer. Even when he'd asked his own fans on Twitter to vote for his next opponent, and gave them a choice between Maidana and myself, and I got twice the number of votes as the Argentine, he'd still picked Maidana. So instead of answering my question he just started shouting and carrying on. I couldn't understand half of what he said and the rest of it – about how much money he was worth, what he made a fight – didn't make sense. What had that got to do with anything? I wasn't going to get drawn into some stupid public slanging match. 'I'm here,' I told him. 'Let's just get on with it and have the fight,' and left it at that. No one's a bigger fan of Floyd Mayweather than me, but people lose respect when they behave like that.

In the meantime, the day-to-day business of being a boxer remained, which meant a fight against Chris Algieri, recently knocked down six times by Manny. It was meant to be a stroll in the park but actually the New Yorker, on his home turf, took me the distance before I won on a unanimous decision. Again, I looked towards Mayweather, and again nothing came in my direction. It was getting a bit stupid. In all honesty I could only think that again he was running scared. How else do you explain his lack of engagement? I genuinely think he could see I had the speed, power and tactical awareness to beat him. Don't get me wrong, it would have been a hell of an achievement, and I'd have gone into any fight with Mayweather as a massive underdog, but I really did believe I could properly trouble him.

In all honesty, I thought Mayweather's attitude was embarrassing. What's the point of being a fighter if you're not going to accept a challenge? And so, in the absence of the welterweight clash I wanted, I looked elsewhere. When Canelo's name was mentioned for a tilt at his WBC middleweight title, I think most people thought it was a crazy proposition, a complete mismatch. Straight away some commentators said I was mad. I got where they were coming from. Canelo, a true boxing superstar, was a formidable opponent – only Mayweather had beaten him in nearly fifty fights and that was by a majority decision – and I was fighting at an unfamiliar weight.

My promoter, Oscar De La Hoya, and me felt different. Oscar knew it would be a great spectacle, and I knew it was a chance not only to become a world champion again but to single myself out as the bravest boxer in the field. It was a way to remind the world just who I was. If nothing else I was certainly given credit for aiming high. One pundit said that me beating Canelo would be the biggest win overseas by a British boxer since the welterweight John H. Stracey beat José Nápoles in Mexico City in 1975. I'll be honest, these weren't really names that meant anything to me. And I couldn't help thinking that people were forgetting I was coming off a good run of performances. Plus it is possible to train up to a weight, building muscle mass and gaining strength. But if I was in with a chance of carrying off the biggest shock in forty years, bring it on!

Nothing about the fight was understated, including the brand new spaceship-like arena in Las Vegas. The fact it was scheduled for a Mexican holiday would only add to the carnival atmosphere. No two ways about it, the Mexican nation, the Mexicans in America, and the Mexicans trying to get into America would all be on Canelo's side. Don't forget this fight came just as Donald Trump was declaring Mexicans public enemy number one. To them, Canelo was more than a boxer. He was their representative in a fight for freedom and justice. He looked the part as well. The Canelo that arrived in the ring that night was a bear of a man.

You might wonder why I mention what he looked like on the night. Well, because he was 32 pounds heavier than he had been at the initial weigh-in, and two stones heavier than me. Hydration is a side of boxing that people don't see. A big boxer will dehydrate to meet the weigh-in target and then rebuild until the fight. It's actually a pretty dangerous game. Do it too much or too quickly and you risk not only damaging your performance but also your body. Think of it like a diver coming up to the surface too quickly. It's a totally unnatural thing to do, so you have to take your time. Try and cheat your body and you can get seriously ill.

In Canelo's case it was like I'd seen one fighter at the weigh-in and a completely different one on the night. Size and weight aren't necessarily as big a deal as people think. I've sparred with heavier guys throughout my career. It doesn't mean they're better than you, and a smaller boxer has an advantage with agility. But when I saw Canelo in the ring the thing that struck me more than anything was the size of his back. He looked like he chopped down trees for a living. It didn't affect my confidence, but it was a bit of a *What am I doing here?* moment.

To be honest, though, it didn't seem to make any real difference. I totally outboxed him in the early rounds. His big weapon was his power shots but he never really got near. In the meantime, I scored more heavily with the judges by picking him off with jabs. That's where experience comes in. It's tempting as an underdog to try to knock a champion off his perch, like a KO is your only chance. I had learned as long ago as those fights with Mario Kindelán that patience could be a virtue.

As tends to happen when a fighter realises he's slipping behind, Canelo bit by bit began to show a bit more until in round six he saw the smallest of opportunities and caught me with a big right-hander. I'll tell you now – it wasn't one of those where you're knocked down and are straight back on your feet. This was a proper big hit. Like he'd struck me with something, a club or a brick or a bat. No way could I punch like that – remember I was still basically fighting with a broken hand. Even without that damage, my hands generally could never take that sort of punishment. Canelo could take on a concrete wall and come out on the winning side.

Those who were watching tell me I was unconscious before I hit the canvas. The count didn't even get started before the medical crew were in the ring. Canelo, to his credit, was straight over. He thought I'd twisted my neck when I hit the canvas, but actually all was OK. I soon came back round and was able to reassure everyone I was OK. Of course, I wasn't really. Inside I was distraught. It felt like Garcia all over again. One little mistake and I'd been caught.

With a bit of time I could be a bit more philosophical. OK, I'd lost. That was a major disappointment. But I could – after the check-up at hospital! – hold my head up high. I had shown the type of boxer, and person, I am by getting in the ring with a genius fighter, a legend, and showing no fear of the challenge. People ask me if I regret that fight. The answer will always be no. Like I say, I never became a boxer to pussyfoot around, have forty fights no one remembers, and then retire. I did it because, one, I loved the sport; and two, I see life as an adventure. I want to be in it all the time. I was a fighter at the end of the day. To me that means saying I'm not scared of anyone and I'll fight anyone as well. Every fighter wants to be great and to do so you have to take the biggest challenges. You have to take these massive, massive risks, not only to your career but maybe to your health.

I was chasing the Mayweather clash but he wouldn't fight me. For years and years he just kept pushing me away. That meant that when the Canelo opportunity came I was happy to take it. Everything – the weight, the gloves, the venue – was in his favour. And I said no problem. That was me wanting to be great and me wanting to do something which no one else would ever consider. That was me being brave, looking for a huge landmark win – and I wasn't that far from pulling it off. Oscar, for one, was full of praise despite my defeat. 'He dared to be great,' was how he put it. 'Dared to be great' – another potential title for this book!

'There will not be another middleweight with speed

like Amir Khan's,' he added. I wouldn't be sticking around in that particular division to find out.

Predictably, there were calls for me to retire. Barry Hearn was one of those keen to be heard, saying I was past my 'sell-by-date', although that might have been more because his son Eddie represented the Sheffield fighter Kell Brook, at that point the IBF welterweight champion, and he wanted to stir the pot regarding a potentially lucrative meet-up.

Instead of retirement, I was actually taking a look towards Rio and potentially a revival of my Olympic dream – only this time fighting for Pakistan. With a number of professionals now competing at the Olympics, golfers and tennis players included, the International Boxing Association had voted in favour of allowing pro boxers the same privilege. The British Boxing Board of Control weren't keen on the idea. It came back to the argument against young amateur boxers being thrown into the ring against hardened experienced fighters – the same one I'd had to overcome to get to Athens twelve years earlier.

Pakistan, however, offered a route, although by no means a simple one – Haroon had tried to do the same thing at London 2012 and been barred because he'd already fought for England. In the end the potential chance to actually represent my heritage slipped away.

Time was short and as the Games got nearer I wondered whether my bruising encounter with Canelo was a little too recent to be setting out on the trail of a qualification tournament and then, if successful, a series of fights at the Olympics itself. I'd have really loved to do it, but in the end it was a shot in the dark that silently slipped away.

While the world's greatest sportspeople warmed up for Rio, I found myself in Manchester – and I was glad. My academic career had floundered when I became an overnight sensation in 2004. Now, though, I was about to be awarded a Doctor of Letters by Manchester Metropolitan University for my sporting success and charity work. Yes, that's right, just call me 'Dr Khan' if you see me around! The honour coming from Manchester Met wasn't a random thing. I'd helped to support their 'Mother Tongue Other Tongue' project celebrating cultural diversity and the variety of languages spoken in UK schools. As I posed for the classic picture, holding a scroll in an academic robe, I was reminded again that there is more to life than boxing. It's people, and their futures, that matter at the end of the day.

• • •

Thankfully, I've always had good people around to help me negotiate different elements of my life. Ricky Hatton is one of them. Had things been different we might actually have met in the ring – our careers did overlap – and there was talk of an arena fight at one point. In the end Ricky retired and so it never happened, and I'm kind of glad because more than anything to me he was a friend.

Right from the start he'd always had a word of encouragement for me which developed over the years into more meaningful conversations about the boxing world, dealing with being famous, and life in general. Ricky has had incredible battles to deal with down the years and I was delighted when he overcame his issues with drink and drugs, people taking advantage of him, and became an even better man than he was before. It was the very fact that Ricky had done so much in the ring, and seen so much out of it, that made him the perfect person to go to for advice.

I'd like to have said the same for Prince Naseem who, as a fellow Muslim of Asian heritage, had done his own bit to open the doors to wider participation in boxing. Sadly, Naseem was a harder nut to crack than Ricky. I'll always praise him for his achievements – as a fighter he was just unbelievable – but he could also be selfish. It frustrated me that he could be so stand-offish. I looked at him as a bit of a touchstone – someone who had been there and done it and who might be able to help me along the way. But if anything he was the total opposite.

It's strange. One day it would feel like we were really close friends and then the next he'd be totally cold with me. He just seemed so arrogant. The way I see it, the more successful I got, the more he got a chip on his shoulder. I think seeing how big a name I became hurt him. It didn't need to be like that but that was how it seemed to me. That aloofness has never changed over the years and the last couple of times our paths have crossed I've not even wanted to go over and say hello to him. I saw him at an Anthony Joshua fight in Saudi Arabia and didn't even acknowledge him. It was funny because his sons, who also went into boxing, were waving at me. I used to help train them. They are great lads, and were big fans of mine when I was fighting, but I just felt so far away from Naseem himself.

As it turned out I was about to go through a period of my life where I'd need more support than any other. And of course that just happened to be the time when so many people who I considered my greatest friends and allies would disappear. Some of that I brought on myself, some of it was out of my control, like an avalanche. Whatever the cause, I can honestly say that when it came to the storm about to engulf me I have never felt more alone.

COACHING SESSION 8

Is it a mistake to seek greatness? Or, more realistically, to try to grab something that pretty much everyone else believes to be out of reach?

By now you'll have realised I'm very much of the mindset that 'if you don't try, how will you ever know what you might have achieved?'. The 'no regrets' mindset you might call it. There are risks in that approach. Knockbacks are more or less inevitable which means there is always a requirement to build yourself up again. But if you feel you can roll with those punches then there is actually a world to be explored outside your front door.

OK, you could try boxing, but I'm talking about anything, from acting to music to becoming something in your local community. How do you make yourself do it? By asking what, in all honesty, you have to lose. In boxing it's usually the shape of your nose! In everything else, it's pretty much nothing at all.

ROUND NINE

I never realised when Canelo's right-hander sent me crashing to the floor, but stunned and dazed would pretty much come to describe my life at that time.

Overnight – well, it felt that way – my core support team of my dad, my uncle Taz and my best friend Saj left me. To make matters worse, when I checked my finances I had barely nothing left. I was only just in my thirties. I had a family, a lot of commitments, all kinds of expenses. *Wow!* I thought. *This is what I've put my life on the line for? I've got the rest of my life ahead of me and it's all gone.* I'd taken the biggest fights, fought the biggest names, knowing that one day I could walk away with absolute security, total peace of mind. And now it had all vanished.

Part of me wanted to laugh. Everyone out there thought I had cash sloshing around in my bank account when in reality it was virtually bone dry. Imagine how you'd feel? I'd look at the figure on my laptop again and again, and the same words would go round and round in my head – *Where has all my money gone? How am I going to survive?*

I was a boxer with a broken hand – how does that work? Your hands are the tools of your trade. It's such an extreme injury, like a footballer breaking a leg, a batsman breaking an arm – and just carrying on. I'd had three operations on it and so just from the surgery that hand was all beat up. How was it ever going to heal? I genuinely thought I was never going to fight again. If I couldn't box then how was I going to make any money? Boxers box. Quit and we're down the job centre with everyone else.

I was sent tumbling into the toughest patch of my life, completely overwhelmed by the situation. Mentally, as well as financially, I was broke. I ended up going through what I can see now was a breakdown. I turned against everyone. In my mind, no one was my friend. The way I looked at it, I couldn't trust anyone. I had it in my head that they were all against me – that my family, my uncle, my best friend Saj, had not only wasted my money but had all fucked me over. Actually, scrap that – I had it in my head that everyone had fucked me over.

I desperately needed help, advice, but just didn't know who was on my side. It felt like down the years I'd gone out of my way to be there, financially and practically, for everyone who needed me and now, when I needed them most, no one was helping me back. One by one they'd all disappeared. *They don't want to help me. Why is that? Why? Why?* To me, there was only one answer. *They've walked away because they think I'm done.*

I knew it happened. Once you're finished as a boxer,

people disappear. They don't care. But somehow — foolishly, naively, whatever you want to call it — I never thought it would happen to me.

I thought about the hand problem and the speculation over whether I would ever fight again. The minute the tide turned against me, those same people who couldn't wait to be around me when I was winning had vanished into thin air. Win a fight and the room's full. Lose and the room's empty. I started hating everyone.

I was left staring into an abyss — pretty much literally when it came to the bottomless money pit of the wedding venue in Bolton. I couldn't believe how much money had gone into it — and it was still only half finished! To me, it felt like money I'd earned that hadn't been taken proper care of. Had that money wasted on the wedding hall been invested properly I would have enjoyed a return on it. Instead it felt like I'd been chucking handfuls of £50 notes on to a bonfire, and the flames were now consuming me.

My family had always said that everything they did for me while I was a boxer was to make sure my life would be perfect in the future. I could retire, never have to work again, and yet still have the same great lifestyle. But I looked at the wedding hall and couldn't understand how investing millions of my money had left nothing more than a mess of bricks, mortar and rubble.

Then there were the office costs — ten grand a month.

One time I got an £8,000 bill. I was stunned. Eight grand! I emailed the address on the demand. Turned out it was for a server. This is me, Amir Khan, a fighter, not a small business with multiple employees. Why had eight grand gone on a server? People think, *What's £8,000 to Amir Khan?* But actually £8,000 is a lot of money. Especially at a point in time where it feels like you haven't got any.

I confronted a mate who was working in the office at the time. We had a big argument. 'You need me more than I need you,' he told me, and started smashing up all the equipment. He walked out and that was that. Afterwards, I started thinking about stories about Faryal and my family that had been leaked to the press. Those stories had always quoted a 'source'. Was that him? Was he the source? Was he trying to drive a wedge between me and Faryal? Or her and my family? Or make me and Faryal look bad? My mind was endlessly whirring.

A couple of days later, I got another slap in the face when I got a letter from my friend's lawyer demanding I give him a redundancy payment. After a bit of back and forth I ended up paying him twenty-one grand. I couldn't believe it. The office was a wreck and *I'd* had to shell out. But then again all this was new to me. I was never hands-on in the business that was 'Amir Khan'. My family and friends kept me away from it. I'd relied on certain people to look after my interests while I was away at training camps or fighting and this is what I'd been left with.

In all honesty, it felt like I'd been paying them just to be there. Don't get me wrong, no one was happier than me to be putting food on the table for my family, but it was hard for me not to feel taken advantage of. Maybe there was a time when I'd have kept those frustrations buttoned up inside but now I was older and more independent I couldn't do that. I had to say something, and if a fall-out happened then so be it.

Because I'd never demanded answers before, my family thought it was Faryal directing me to ask questions about the money. To them, she was still the incomer, the new face, who hadn't been there when things were, supposedly, hunky-dory. My family's conclusion? *It must be her causing trouble. She has to be to blame.* That wasn't true. It was me, Amir, a grown-up, a father even. I was concerned about my family's future. I'd sweated, not to mention spilt blood, to get to this position. It wasn't unreasonable of me to want to know what was happening. I had to think of my future. I couldn't just let this situation – money spewing out of my account – roll on and on. Where would that leave me in five years? Ten?

Changes had to be made. I sacked everyone who was left working for me – and again Faryal got the blame. Apparently, she was the one making me do this stuff, like I was a puppet on a string, when that wasn't the case at all. I'd realised changes needed to be made, and that's what I did.

Faryal, meanwhile, is a strong woman and wasn't going to just sit back and let my family bad-mouth her. I might be the one who wears the boxing gloves but she's perfectly capable of defending her corner, and she did just that. After my parents publicly criticised her choice of 'immodest' clothes, for example, she promptly stuck a naked photo of Haroon at a party on Snapchat. Try being the one in the middle of that! But there was more to what Faryal was pointing out than simple double standards. By taking on my family in public she wanted to open up a wider debate about the way son's wives can so often be treated as outsiders, second-class citizens almost, in Muslim families – ostracised, abused and even worse.

It was a bad fall-out, no two ways about it. While to my family Faryal was the enemy, she was the only person I trusted. Me and her versus everyone else. At a really horrible time, when all I wanted was to draw the curtains and lie in the dark, she gave me the motivation to battle on. I was so thankful to her for everything she did for me when I felt everyone else had turned their backs. It was a lonely place to be – and then I made it even lonelier by ostracising her as well.

· · ·

The catalyst for this new nightmare was a meeting at a friend's house in Dubai – both me and Faryal were there. Afterwards I felt there was a possibility of a sponsorship deal in the offing. As I've said, our money situation wasn't great and so, while Faryal went home, I stayed on.

Our host had a few friends round and invited me for a dip in his pool. There were about six of us in the water, including a couple of girls, and we chatted while we had a drink. A picture subsequently found its way on to social media. When Faryal saw it, her reaction was clear – I had stayed there to party and hang out with girls. I tried to clear the air. 'Faryal, no. It looks worse than it is!' – one of those sentences 100 per cent guaranteed to make things worse!

By way of revenge, she sent me a picture of a message supposedly from the former world heavyweight champion Anthony Joshua showing that they were going to meet up. It was all a bit silly looking back, but I get it – she wanted to hurt me the way I'd hurt her. Predictably enough, bearing in mind my mental state at the time – feeling ripped off, the wedding hall, the mangled hand, probably never being able to fight again – I lost it.

I knew Faryal liked Joshua. She isn't a fan of boxing, but from seeing him on TV she appreciated that he was kind and respectful. When I asked her about it, she confirmed she was going to meet him. She said he was a better man than me and he was going to take her for dinner. Obviously, I found that totally disrespectful. I had only one thought – to lash out. I took all the stress I was under and turned it on my wife – and Joshua.

I grabbed my phone and went straight to Twitter – *Lol moved up in the weight classes lol. Trust me I ain't the jealous type. No need to send me pictures of the men you're talking to #Disgusted.*

I wasn't finished. *Left my family and friends for this Faryal. I'm not hurt but another fighter? I'm making it public. You getting the divorce #Golddigger.*

Mans like Joshua, I added, *can have my leftovers!*

She had pushed my buttons good and proper, particularly the one marked 'DETONATE!' All I could think was how, just a few weeks beforehand, me and Joshua had been to Germany together to launch a computer game, and now this. It made it even more disrespectful. What I should have done is think it through – was it really likely that Joshua was carrying on with Faryal? Instead I'd gone straight to social media.

It wasn't long before I had a call from Joshua. 'Listen, I don't know what you're talking about. I haven't done anything wrong. I've not spoken to your wife. Why have you brought my name into this? I don't even know who she is. I have respect for you. I would never do that. I can't believe you put my name out there.'

He made it clear that he hadn't been in contact with Faryal, but that didn't mean I had to believe it.

'Go fuck yourself,' I told him, and put the phone down. On Twitter he put out the video of the Shaggy song 'It Wasn't Me'.

Until your life becomes a soap opera, played out on social media, it's hard to comprehend what it's like. Worse, by getting in that pool I'd started the whole storyline. It was tough, really tough, and then of course it was all over the papers. The damage was done, was getting worse and worse, and I couldn't see any way back for Faryal and me.

I actually told her 'I'm going to divorce you.' In my religion, say that three times and it's legal. I did just that. Except there was one thing I didn't know at the time. Faryal was pregnant. That meant my saying 'I divorce you' was void. A man cannot divorce a wife who is pregnant. Hearing a baby was on the way was a moment of absolute clarity – I saw how selfish I'd been. In so many ways our daughter, Alayna, was our saviour – the best blessing we ever had. We were going to split up. Instead, not only did we stay together but we had a beautiful little girl.

At that point I knew it was time for me to put an end to my stupid behaviour. Faryal had only gone down the route of talking about Joshua because she had a trust issue with me. Nothing might have happened in the pool, but there had been girls in the past and all that had to stop. I'd become a bad person. I'd lost sight of who I was and what I really wanted. Things had gone way too far. I apologised to Faryal. Not just any apology, but from the heart. Faryal had been the one person who'd always been there for me. She'd been strong for me, and I had no right to treat her the way I had.

It serves me right that even to this day I get people making jokes about the Joshua thing. Worse than that, it looked like the friendship I had with him was bust for ever. I'd always enjoyed being around Joshua. We were united by that joint experience of reaching the pinnacle of our sport after being Olympians. We'd shared good times but the truth is we didn't speak for a long period after my tweets. I don't blame him. At the end of the day, I put him in the line of fire for no reason. Any hope that he might forgive and forget seemed to end when, five years on, someone on Twitter asked him: 'AJ lad did you fuck Mrs. Khan back in the day?'

'Honestly,' he replied. 'I didn't. With all the accusations around me name. I wish I did.'

I took the joke on the chin, and it hurt. So you can understand my relief when we met recently in Dubai, talked things over and agreed to bury the hatchet.

• • •

No matter how much I tried to move forward, it seemed like new lows lurked round every corner. At one point a 'sex tape' was leaked to the press. It was from before I was married, before I was a father, but it was clearly put out there by someone trying to cause me a lot of hurt, to make me look bad and untrustworthy. The thing that bothered me most was how it would affect my charity work. Would anyone want to collaborate with me again?

I had my suspicions about where it had come from, who might have had this old footage, and why they'd chosen this moment to send it to a tabloid, but it wasn't something I could prove and again I just had to do my best to deal with the damage. I was in America at the time and it was hard to get an angle on just how badly this was damaging my reputation in the UK, but truth is I was scared to go back home for a while. All I could do was defend myself from across the Atlantic, and at one point me and Faryal even did a live link-up with Phillip Schofield and Holly Willoughby on ITV's *This Morning* to try to explain how really the sex tape was a non-story, something that had come back to haunt me from the past, and wasn't relevant to our relationship or anything else going on in my life at that time.

I'm sure this isn't something that happens in most people's lives, and if anyone's wondering what it's like to have a sex tape flying around on the internet I can definitely say it's not very nice. Let's just say I was glad my dad never asked me about it – what could I have said to him? I know it wasn't something I was keen to sit down and watch with him! All I could really do was put it down as another learning curve, but it caused me a lot of pain as I'm a private person and, as someone who prides himself on being a role model, I didn't want anyone to think a sex tape in some way signified what I was like. As everyone does at some point, I'd made a mistake. The difference was mine was shown across the world.

Looking back, I can see how suffocated I was during that whole massive family fall-out. I'd always been very strong mentally, always felt there was nothing I couldn't deal with, but I really did feel the weight of the world on top of me. It was the most alone I've ever been and I had no idea what to do. I'll be honest, there were occasions when the only thing keeping me going was my kids. Thinking about them and their future was the only focus I had. That's why I describe the reality show *I'm a Celebrity . . . Get Me Out of Here!* in a different way to pretty much anyone else who's ever been on it – it was a lifesaver.

My trust in everyone and everything had been shattered and so, at a time when everything else was going pear-shaped, when the offer came my way I thought *Why not?* A few weeks in a jungle on the other side of the world seemed like the ideal way to have a break from the never-ending turbulence of the real world. To get away for three weeks, totally uncontactable, just me and my thoughts? It was like someone had thrown me a lifebelt.

Thing was, I had no idea what *I'm a Celebrity* was about. I'd never seen it, and it was only a couple of weeks before the flight from the UK that I found out the show had a habit of locking contestants in coffins full of snakes and shoving their heads in little round bowls full of spiders. As anyone who knows me will tell you, I'm not a big fan of snakes, spiders, or any kind of creepy-crawly. The thought of being buried underground with 2,000 cockroaches was more than I could take. Escape from the misery of my reality or not, I made up my mind to pull out. Having already made myself look stupid with the accusations about Joshua, I couldn't bear the thought of now making myself look a wimp on one of the biggest shows on TV. I just wanted somehow to get back to what I knew – boxing.

A late pull-out was the last thing ITV wanted, to the extent that the head of the channel travelled all the way up to Bolton to try to change my mind.

'Look,' she said, 'this will be really good for you. It will let people see another side of you – the real side.' I knew she was referring to all the negative press. 'People will see you,' she told me, 'and hear you.'

Maybe that was true, or maybe, thinking a bit more

cynically, ITV thought I was the sort of person who'd hook up with a girl. With me being Muslim, that kind of bad behaviour would be emphasised even more. There was also the chance I'd talk about my inner feelings. They knew I was all over the place emotionally, falling out with my family. I understood their agenda but a part of me also thought that approach a little sly, which made me more determined not to give in to them. Either way, to see one of the hardest men in Britain shrieking at the sight of a spider? They knew they were going to get their money's worth with me. One way or another, I was an accident waiting to happen, which was why presumably I was one of the highest-paid contestants in the history of the show, getting even more than Katie Price.

I hadn't expected the ITV boss to convince me, but the more I listened, the more I thought: *You know what? The way things are I've got nothing to lose.* Also, she emphasised that while, yes, there would be snakes and spiders, no one was going to get hurt.

She was right. While the TV show itself is action-packed, the truth of the matter is there's an awful lot of sitting around doing nothing. Again, perfect for me. While I lay in camp, I used that time to work out exactly what I wanted – to create a long-term future with my wife, to be with my kids, to be a family man. I knew I'd made mistakes messing about with different women, same as I had accusing my wife of being unfaithful. The jungle gave me an opportunity to think, whereas on the outside people would constantly be telling me, 'Do this! Do that!' – I couldn't think for myself out there. The barrier that *I'm a Celebrity* created was a blessing. It made me realise what I wanted and didn't want in life.

Yes, there was still that boisterous side to me, and I expect another reason ITV wanted me on the show was there was a decent chance I would do something daft. As someone who's spent his life in front of cameras, I soon became totally oblivious to them being around. It never really occurred to me that there were millions of people watching me, which is probably why I became embroiled in one of the show's most infamous moments – 'Strawberry-gate'. This was when me and fellow contestant, the DJ Iain Lee, went off to do a Dingo Dollar Challenge – basically a chance to win a treat for our hungry team-mates back in camp.

We completed the task and were rewarded with a bowlful of juicy strawberries and a jug of cream. We headed back to camp, but then Iain came up with the suggestion that we secretly eat them ourselves. There was a bit of a discussion (OK, not much) about the rights and wrongs of the situation, and I was worried that the other contestants were bound to find out, but in the end me and Iain did exactly that. It was funny at the time, especially since I was dressed in a cat costume – quite literally the cat who got the cream, licking it off my paws – but straight away I started feeling bad and was sorry I'd done it.

Back at the camp we owned up. Dennis Wise, the former Wimbledon and Chelsea hardman, in particular wasn't very happy about it, and neither were the others. It wasn't so much that they were hungry, it was more that it was a bit of a sad thing to do. That was the worst thing about it – that there was so much love in the camp and then we'd gone and done that. Me being me, I put most of the blame on Iain and he got it worse than me, but I did feel scared that I'd ruined the atmosphere. I didn't want that to happen at all.

In the jungle, you have no idea what's happening back in the UK, and only when I was voted out did I realise just how big an issue Strawberry-gate was, all over the tabloids for days. Back on home soil, me and Iain were quizzed about it endlessly, even given the third degree by Piers Morgan on *Good Morning Britain*.

We laugh about it now. Iain had worked in the media for a long time and had twigged straight away that us eating the strawberries would make great TV. But I never for one moment thought how big that moment would be in my life. Even now I get people asking questions about it. I'm like, 'It was a long time ago – give me a break!' At least people have forgotten my other gaffe on the show when I asked: 'Has there ever been a female Prime Minister?' – when the PM at the time was actually Theresa May. Well, they'd forgotten it until I just reminded them now!

Strawberry-gate dominated everyone else's memories of my time on the show but, when I viewed a wider selection of clips after I came out, I saw behind the charade of silliness. I saw myself as what I was – someone who just needed time away from real life.

And it worked. Lying on my bunk, I concluded how much I had to thank Faryal for. I thought of her alone, pregnant, and with another child to look after, picking them up and dropping them off at school, plus all the other day-to-day stuff of being a parent, with no help at all. I thought of what it must be like to be married to someone always in the papers, and to carry the strain of the same financial pressure. Faryal has never needed me for money – she's a successful businesswoman in her own right – but equally a large part of our future financial security had disappeared. One minute she was with someone with big money, and now there was hardly anything left.

I knew I was so lucky to have her, how much she'd invested in me. I thought about how we'd got engaged when she was still a baby, a teenager, and I'd brought her from America to a new life in Bolton where she'd had to get used to being constantly 'papped', everyone wanting a look at her. What must that have been like? While we had got ourselves back on track before I travelled to Australia, I wanted to properly say I understood; to say sorry.

The jungle was where I sorted myself out, where the negativity stopped. It opened my eyes to what could happen, what I could lose, if I carried on being angry and bitter. It allowed me to put the jigsaw of my life – scattered in a thousand pieces on the floor – back together. I took a look at myself and saw someone who could be selfish and hard-headed; someone who needed to think with his heart and his head instead of with his ego. I could keep digging myself a deeper and deeper hole or I could start trying to do things differently. I set my goals for the next four or five years – where I wanted to be, how I wanted to do things. I knew I had to repair the relationship with my family, and also get back into big-time boxing, the sorts of fights that would make me big money, replace the massive amount that had gone missing, and properly set me and my family up for life.

I'm not saying that was easy. There would have to be a lot of forgiving and forgetting. I was still hurt and confused about the money. I fell out with my family because I felt I'd been used and abused. I genuinely did feel I'd been taken advantage of. On the other hand, I'd lost enough people from my life without adding them too. The money was gone and that was that. Until this day I haven't questioned it, and I'll carry on that way.

Looking back, using an independent financial adviser from the start would have saved a lot of turmoil. But we were a close family and so we did it our way, the result, probably inevitably, being this huge internal explosion. I mean, imagine falling out with your family, who've said some pretty bad stuff about your wife, she's retaliated, a black hole of a construction project is sucking up vast amounts of money, and it feels like other finances are disappearing to who knows where. It was killing me. Every day I felt like I was ageing a year. White hairs appeared in my beard overnight.

I was in crisis and couldn't help thinking of some of the big names of the past who'd been on top of the world and somehow ended up with nothing. There's a long list of fighters who have made fortunes only to lose the lot. I'd sat with Mike Tyson as he told me how it had happened to him. He instilled in me how important it is to have good people around you, people you can trust. It's a brave man who rips off Mike Tyson. But it happens to the best of them – and I didn't want to be the next. I also came to realise eventually that bitterness eats you up. I had to let it go.

This all happened ten years ago, and I spoke about it in the press at the time. I've moved on since then. Looking back, I know I should have paid more attention to my finances. Regardless of the rights and wrongs of it all, I can only tell you how I felt back then.

I've learned so much about myself in the past few years, mainly independence. Beforehand, I had a whole team of people to do everything for me. They took me here, there and everywhere. Even told me what to wear. Sounds mad, but it's only recently I've started travelling on the train on my own. Same with cars. I'd always have someone to drive me. Not any more. Now I'm my own man.

I like being in charge of my own life, finally being the boss. Because success came to me so young I'd never had that chance. Aged seventeen, I might have been Olympic champion, but I was still living at home being told what to do. I became used to that, never questioned it. As I got older, it was only natural that my family should control everything, including my finances, my diary. Even if I wasn't happy with something I'd still do it, because that's the way it was. I was like a robot at times. The alternative wasn't even in my head. Remember as well, in a strong Muslim family, it's only natural to follow your father's leadership. Rebellion? Forget it. It's not that you don't want to upset the apple cart; it's more that the thought of upsetting the apple cart isn't even there. Eventually, I did start doing some things differently, the biggest one being marrying outside the family. But there was a limit to how far I'd go. I kept a lot of people close, and eventually it became suffocating.

Even now I have a lot of friends who, at my age, do everything their parents say. I listen to my mum and dad, but I will still make my own decisions, even if they're not happy with it. Money can buy a lot of things. In my case it helped me become my own man, but it also very nearly caused me to lose everything.

. . .

Over the following months, as I started to train and fight again, those same people who had disappeared in my time of need started to drift back. And because I'm a good guy, with a good heart, I forgave them and let them back into the picture. God had given me a second chance and so I gave them a second chance too. They might have thought nothing had changed – same old Amir – but I knew different. Inside, I'd made a vow – *I'm going to be smarter this time. I'm not going to attach myself to people like I used to. I'm going to think of me and my family.*

More than anything I was going to think of Faryal. As a boxer I was broken. She was the one who helped me get my feet back on the ground, even going so far as to organise one of the training camps. She could so easily have walked away. Instead, she saw I was struggling mentally and gave me some solid ground where all around me was quicksand. On that little island of sanity we slowly rebuilt.

I was reminded of the me of a few years back when, in 2022, I returned to *I'm a Celebrity* for a special 'all stars' show, this time swapping Australia for South Africa, alongside some of the programme's most memorable participants. I couldn't help thinking how I was a different person. I had no distractions. No longer was I stressing. I was happy. I remembered those terrible few months of five years earlier. How, from the outside, people must have thought: *He's Amir Khan, he's a world champion boxer, a superstar – he must have everything he wants*, when really I had nothing. It gives me strength now to think that I did eventually overcome that time.

I would also, finally, make, and keep, some money. From a professional career of forty fights, only from the last four would I have something to show for my efforts. Those are the fights which secured me and my family for the rest of my life. I made double what I lost.

But those battles would come at a different kind of cost.

COACHING SESSION 9

When everything seems lost, you have to carry on. There have been times in my life where I've felt so desperate I'd have been happy if a hole appeared and swallowed me up. It looked like everything I really treasured in life had vanished, never to be seen again. Sometimes, as you can see in this chapter, I've brought those events on myself. Other times they've exploded in my face.

I'll tell you now that the only way to keep going forward is forgiveness — that might be of yourself or of others. We all make mistakes. If we let them chew us up for the rest of our lives then we'll never get anywhere.

ROUND TEN

After the Canelo defeat, I knew if I was to carry on I'd have to finally address the issue of my hand injury. Declining powers are bad enough without only being able to punch at 40 per cent. I also didn't want to persevere with the endless pain that made training feel so negative in my mind. The operation, however, was complex. Bone was taken from my hip and grafted on to my hand. The whole lot was held together with a bunch of metal pins. When I looked at the X-ray I thought I was seeing an advert for the Screwfix catalogue.

Undoubtedly, after the surgery I was in much better condition. But as one thing was mended, another was falling apart. The problem was my heart. I just didn't have the passion for the sport any more. In the ring, I'd achieved my ambition, been world champion. Outside the ring I'd met and married Faryal and got a young family. All the big boxes had been ticked. I didn't see the sport in the same way. It was no longer my everything like it had been. The love was gone.

Trouble was I had a wedding hall to finish and a bank account to fill. The hall would cost me another £3 million. By the end it would cost me £12.5 million. Thankfully, boxing is a sport of smoke and mirrors. When it comes to demanding seven-figure sums for fights, no one can see the fire in your belly is slowly going out.

My own worries were again dwarfed by what was happening around me. In May 2017, an Islamist extremist suicide bomber set off a bomb as thousands of people, mainly young girls, were leaving an Ariana Grande concert at Manchester Arena, just a few miles down the road from Bolton, and a place where I had fought numerous times. Twenty-three people were killed, the youngest just eight years old, and hundreds more injured. I was actually driving into Manchester at the time, confused by how traffic was backing up out of the city centre and the sheer number of police and emergency vehicles around. I ended up in a café which was when I started to hear reports of the explosion. I couldn't believe it. Here? In Manchester? On my own doorstep? I felt sick at the thought of it – the violence, the hurt and the devastation. How could anyone do something like that?

I was transported back to 2005 and the horror of the bombings on 7/7, and like then I talked publicly about how important it was to identify and combat extremism. I went on *Good Morning Britain* and encouraged people to report any extremism they might hear, any twisting of Islam into something hideous and aggressive.

For me, there was a big difference between the Manchester bombing and 7/7 – this time I was a father myself. I looked at my daughter and saw how the fallout of extremism could affect her in the future, how people might point the finger at her, call her names, say horrible things. I knew that was likely – it had already happened to friends of mine. I hated the way the actions of one person could be so divisive, could cause a lifetime of hurt for so many others.

'This is against my religion,' I told the programme. 'In the Quran it doesn't say you should kill innocent people. This is something we're all against.'

I don't know if it ever makes any difference me doing these kinds of things, but you never know. When you see an atrocity like that happen where you live you will do anything in your power to try to ensure it never happens again.

. . .

While for the families of those murdered on that awful night the clock no doubt stopped right there and then, everyone else's world kept spinning. As fate turned out my first fight back, against the Canadian, Phil Lo Greco, made it look like I was firing on all available cylinders. Within a minute he was knocked out on the canvas at Liverpool's Echo Arena. Afterwards, the questions, as ever, were all about a big UK showdown with Kell Brook.

As far as I was concerned that fight could wait. It was bound to happen as there was so much money to be made from the rivalry, but in the meantime I was looking elsewhere.

While Lo Greco might have stung like a butterfly and floated like a bee, I do still get asked about one memorable element of the clash. At the press conference, he decided to start mouthing off about the whole Anthony Joshua business. Lots of stuff that isn't really meant is said on these occasions, but I felt that was a low blow. There's a few unwritten rules about press conferences, and not bringing family into it is one of them. 'Don't punch your opponent' is another, but I did have a glass in front of me. I'm glad I stopped myself throwing it, but I did chuck the contents in his face. People said it was a set-up, a cheap way of getting publicity for the fight. I promise that wasn't the case. I actually shocked myself that I'd done it. It was weird, like I was watching myself from the crowd. But if you think about what I'd been through in the previous few months, all the drama before I'd gone into the jungle, the stuff in the media, I just flipped. I just wasn't going to take it any more. He was basically bringing Faryal into the picture when she wasn't there to defend herself. *Fuck you*, I thought, *I'm not having that.*

The fact the Lo Greco fight was so short meant the watching world never saw the truth of what I knew inside – there had been a fairly obvious deterioration since I was knocked out by Canelo. People knew me as a fast fighter, an explosive fighter – a big-hearted guy who could cause people damage. But the time comes when that disappears. With age it goes. And when it does, that affects you mentally as well as physically.

Throughout my whole career, I was always excited to go into a fight. All I'd think about was getting out there and putting on a performance. But a few months later, when I took on the Colombian, Samuel Vargas, in Birmingham, I knew I was properly on a downward trajectory.

For me, Vargas was the fight that really confirmed my declining powers. I remember it vividly. I just couldn't get to him, missing by inches where normally I would have caught him. At the same time, his shots were still hitting me. My timing was out by a second. That was what age, wear and tear was doing to me. And in boxing, if your timing is out by a second that's a big deal. A second can see you blinking for daylight on the floor, and in fact Vargas did drop me at the end of the second round. Thankfully, I did the same to him twice, and won the fight on points by some distance.

It was a bittersweet victory. While the surgery on my hand helped, I still felt compromised. It was never going to be the same as it was when it was in perfect condition.

There's no such thing as a miracle cure. Even now in cold weather that hand hurts. I sit next to someone at dinner and I can see them looking at the scars. There was something else. With my right hand fixed I'd been hitting harder against Lo Greco, which then caused me issues with my elbow and shoulder. Think about it, I'd been holding back on that hand for the best part of thirty fights and then all of a sudden I'd started pushing it again. Look at my arms and the left is more developed than the right. People actually think I'm left-handed!

Boxers carry injuries. There's always something. We're never at 100 per cent. But as you get older coping with those injuries gets so much harder. Training gets harder. Fighting gets harder. One injury goes and another comes along. When you're younger, you can work through them. As time goes on, the drive to continually be overcoming one setback or another disappears. For me, it was like I was less hungry. I didn't want to have to keep working through niggle after niggle, pain after pain. I didn't want to keep having to enter that dark tunnel and battle towards the light.

In truth, the Vargas fight had shocked me. I'm my own biggest critic and my thought process was even clearer than before – *From this point on I need to get the biggest fights I can and then cash out.* I was no longer at what to me was an acceptable level. The gulf was widening

I'm a Celebrity, 2017. While I lay in camp, I used that time to work out exactly what I wanted — to create a long-term future with my wife, to be with my kids, to be a family man.

(*Below*) I returned to *I'm a Celebrity* in 2022 for a special 'all stars' show, this time swapping Australia for South Africa.

I describe the show in a different way to pretty much anyone else who's ever been on it — it was a lifesaver.

Since March 2021, *Meet the Khans* has been good for our relationship. The show is very much about myself and Faryal and so forces us together a lot of the time.

I find it odd to be labelled a reality TV star when I've always thought of myself as a boxer, but I know as well that it's good not to be forever trapped in your past.

Faryal and I on set during a campaign shoot for Faryal Beauty.

My family have been my foundation for everything I have achieved . . .

Celebrating with my Uncle Taz (*left*) and Dad (*right*).

2022. Eid with my son Zaviyar.

With my daughters Lamaisah (*top*) and Alayna (*right*).

I had to deal with the devastating news that Mum had been diagnosed with stage two pancreatic cancer . . . She was the absolute rock around which everyone's world revolved. Thankfully, after months of anguish we were able to see our prayers had been answered and she was on the road to recovery.

Knowing the peace and direction Islam gave me meant my mates respected my religion.

2018. Faryal and I with the former Prime Minister of Pakistan, and cricketing hero, Imran Khan.

We're English, we're British, but that connection with Pakistan will always be there.

Through boxing, I have met some legends of the sport. *From top to bottom*: Terence Crawford, Souleymane Cissokho, Evander Holyfield, Kostya Tszyu, Roy Jones Jr., Mike Tyson, Muhammad Ali and Oleksandr Usyk.

I have had the privilege to meet some incredible people (including royalty) during my life and career. *From top to bottom, below and opposite*: Her Late Majesty Queen Elizabeth II, Their Royal Highnesses the Prince and Princess of Wales, Jay Z, Kendall Jenner, Erik ten Hag, Cristiano Ronaldo, Mr. T, Sir Bobby Charlton, Ashley Young, Rio Ferdinand and Michael Carrick.

The Amir Khan Foundation (established in 2014). I wanted to set up an organisation that not only was ready to respond to disasters but would help struggling people and communities in the UK and across the world.

I'm a spiritual person. God has helped me and instilled in me a belief in helping others.

between where I was now and where I was ten years before. But if my position in the sport meant I could make more money than I could ten years ago, why not take it? That's how boxing works. It's not necessarily the best versus the best, it's which fight will create the biggest pot of money for everyone to dip into. We're boxers, but we're also prize fighters.

. . .

There was one fight which offered more than most – the undefeated WBO welterweight champion, Terence Crawford, viewed as one of the leading pound-for-pound boxers in the world, in front of almost 20,000 baying spectators at the mecca of world boxing, Madison Square Garden in New York. I thought of all the iconic battles of the past that had happened in that vast indoor bowl – the 'Fight of the Century', Muhammad Ali versus Joe Frazier, which I'd seen so many times on video; Rocky Marciano versus Joe Louis; Evander Holyfield and Lennox Lewis. Some places live and breathe sporting history and, in boxing, Madison Square Garden is top of the tree.

The fight venue fitted me perfectly. I love New York, had married a girl from there, and had always been on the radar of US boxing fans. I knew the vast majority of the crowd would be shouting for Crawford, but, if anything,

I've always relished having my back to the wall. No one gave me a cat in hell's chance. I wasn't stupid. I understood that Crawford's team saw me as an easy option, an ageing ex-champion who was over the hill. But actually Crawford himself was past his best at that time. We were pretty much the same age. No fight is over before the bell is rung. Anyone can take their eye off the prize, make a mistake, and in that moment they're gone.

Maybe I was being optimistic – some bookies had me at 30/1! That didn't stop a massive amount of hype. I'd been around a while at that point, travelled the world. Sometimes you think you've seen it all, nothing can catch you by surprise, but seeing my face lit up on one of those massive billboards in Times Square was something else. For the second time, I was also invited to ring the opening bell at the Nasdaq Stock Market, having previously done so for the Paulie Malignaggi fight, also at Madison Square Garden, but in its smaller venue, The Theater.

I've never been nervous walking out for a fight. If anything, I've always revelled in the spotlight. I love the whole razzmatazz – lights flashing, music blaring, compère bigging the whole thing up, crowd going mad. What's not to like? But Madison Square Garden was different level. It's not so much the scale – although it is massive – it's the atmosphere that comes from so much boxing history having happened there. As ever, you're in the moment, but at the same time you can't help feeling you're part of something bigger, a chapter in a never-ending story.

There was something else about Madison Square Garden. Boxing is a weird sport. For months building up to a fight you're surrounded by people, barely a second to yourself, and then, right at the end, you're totally on your own. That's how it has to be, obviously – it's not like you can have your trainer dancing around the ring – but Madison Square Garden highlighted it even more starkly. The bell went and as chants of 'USA, USA' echoed through the auditorium, that was it – everything was on me.

Some sportspeople try to offset a moment like that through visualisation. You see it with cricketers, practising shots out in the middle, facing an imaginary bowler, before the start of play. That way, when the big moment actually comes, it's already in their memory bank. The weapon of surprise is dulled.

I was shown these kinds of techniques before the Olympics, but it wasn't something I liked to do. Not only was it boring but it was tricky in boxing to find that moment to yourself. For days in the run-up, there's always people in and around the ring, sorting electrics out, cameras, all sorts. If anything, my way was precisely the opposite of visualisation. I'd try to enjoy a bit of quiet time and not think about what was coming up. I know it sounds weird considering how big some of my fights were, but for me it was always, *Nah, I'll just get in there and do it!*

I took myself off again to the peace and quiet of Virgil Hunter's gym near San Francisco to prepare for the fight. I knew that taking myself away from distraction was always a good move for me, a view reinforced by a recent chat with Mike Tyson, where he'd told me how his career had headed towards a black hole when the pull of celebrity had become a distraction. In Mike's case he became suffocated by people who were bad for him and clearly took advantage. 'You have to be selfish,' he told me. And I knew exactly what he was saying.

The first round against Crawford was cagey. He made himself hard to hit but I'd trained hard and felt I was doing OK. That was until Crawford caught me with a right-hander and I stumbled to the canvas. The hit hadn't really damaged me, but as the fight went on Crawford began to dominate. Again my timing was out and again I couldn't judge the reach. He was catching me when he shouldn't and I wasn't catching him when I should. Truth was he wasn't hitting me because he was good, he was hitting me because my time was done.

Cuts to my face showed the punishment I was taking and then, in the sixth round, Crawford caught me with a short punch below the belt, his left hand slamming into my groin. The pain was unbelievable. I couldn't breathe and the fight was stopped while I clung on to the ropes, head down, gasping for air. In a low-blow situation like this, so long as the referee deems it an accident, a boxer gets five minutes recovery time, but I was in so much pain that particular rule barely registered. It didn't really matter. I probably could have continued. But I was getting badly hit. I was tiring and the below-the-belt strike had weakened me even more. I'd made the money. Did I need to go back in and take a load more punishment? *You know what*, I thought, *I'm going to call it*. Virgil threw in the towel.

I got a lot of shit for that decision. Boos rang round. The crowd weren't impressed and neither were the journalists and commentators. Everyone said the same thing – 'He wasn't up for it. He took the easy way out.'

Maybe they were right. But judgement comes easy when it's entertainment, something watched from a seat in the crowd. Remember, we're real people down in that ring. I've got massive respect for all boxing fans. They're the ones who put me where I am. But equally they're not the person who has to go back into the ring when they're feeling barely alive; they're not the one taking the punishment – punishment which, let's face it, is only going to get a lot worse. As Virgil Hunter put it after the fight: 'The crowd will always be bloodthirsty and want to see a dramatic ending but you have to look out for the safety of the fighter.'

Remember, boxing is a sport. We're not in there to kill or maim one another. No fighter should feel outside pressure to stay in the ring when obviously it's all over and there's a chance of serious injury. It's not a test of how big an alpha male you are to do that. It's just crazy. At some point a boxing career comes to an end. Should the rest of a fighter's life be lived with brain damage or early onset dementia? We've all heard the phrase 'punch drunk'. Well, we're the sport where it came from. There's plenty of fighters out there with poor memories, or slurred speech. I wasn't just Amir Khan any more – I was Amir Khan, husband and dad. I wanted to walk away from the sport on my own terms. And that's the way I looked at it. *Is this about me going back in there and taking a beating? Or is it about me being smart?* My internal answer was clear. *I've had enough. Now it's time to step back.*

It was the first time I'd ever felt like that, but I didn't surprise myself. Quitting that fight might have been wrong, but it was also the right call at the time. Paulie Malignaggi, a pundit on the night, got it spot on when he noted: 'Khan just needed a moment to be done. That was his moment.'

Fight or flight? I chose flight. Of course, I didn't admit

that back then. 'I have never quit from anything. I would rather be knocked out,' I insisted after the fight. Crawford was unconvinced, claiming he'd hit me in the leg. I didn't know whether to laugh or cry. In the leg? It was in the balls! I also thought, but didn't say, *What would have happened if it had been the other way round? If I'd hit him in the balls with an illegal shot?* I knew the answer. There'd have been an outcry. I'd have been disqualified. I'd still have been the bad guy, the cheat – sometimes you just can't win. As the great boxing analyst Steve Bunce noted: 'I've seen fighters in small halls getting thrown out for shots like that, accidental or intentional.' No way was that going to happen here.

· · ·

Crawford urged me to 'tell the truth'. OK, here goes. Truth is the fight was a payday, a chance to earn big money – a $10 million step on my quest to make myself secure. But if you think I walked away from that fight with a sly smile on my face, fresh as a daisy, take a look at some of the pictures. I was beat up. I had to go to hospital because after that low hit 'in the leg' I was pissing blood. I'd not have bothered – blood in the urine happens sometimes – but Faryal insisted. Looking out for me, as ever.

I knew also I needed to walk away from my entire

career. I had to think about my retirement now not later. My speed was dropping. I was falling short on punches. Training had become a chore. No longer did I feel like I had it in me. From that point on, all I was interested in was the inevitable cash-out fight against Kell. I say 'inevitable' because Kell was always going to be the cash-out. Everyone knew it, including Kell. He couldn't wait to tell anyone who'd listen that I'd quit against Crawford, thereby adding even more fizz to our fight.

Before Kell, though, I wanted to have another fight quickly to get my confidence back. There was a bit more to it than that. The plan was for me to fight the WBC Asian champion, Neeraj Goyat, making it the first pro clash between a fighter of Pakistani heritage and an Indian fighter. I liked the idea a lot. With my own history of bringing people together in the UK, I looked at the potential of us meeting in the ring, respecting each other, and thought maybe this could help the same thing happen on an international level. Me and Neeraj were the perfect people to do that. The first Indian boxer to have made it to the WBC world rankings, he was a hero in his country. I was an icon in Pakistan.

The fight had another angle. One of the first of its kind, it was to be staged in Saudi Arabia. Sadly, with just a few weeks to go, Neeraj was involved in a car accident. His injuries meant he couldn't fight and so the Australian,

Billy Dib, stepped into the fray. I was bigger than Dib, stronger than him, and more experienced. He was also lacking fitness and clearly on the downward slide. Basically, it was a mismatch in my favour – Dib was routinely dispatched in four rounds – but, importantly, the win gave me back some of the buzz I'd been missing. It also meant a lot to me to fight in Saudi Arabia, an important place of pilgrimage for Muslims.

It's easy to think, particularly with personal events outside the ring becoming so dominant in these later years of my career, that I had taken my eye off the ball when it came to external religious, social and political issues. But that was never true. After the Dib fight, for example, I headed east to stand alongside the people of Kashmir and call for peace in the ongoing dispute with India. I vowed to spread the word about the brutality being endured by Kashmiris, who I felt were living under siege at that time. I had a role to play as a prominent voice and I wasn't going to shirk it. Situations like this were another reason why I had set up my foundation. Funds could go directly to those who were suffering.

I went to Kashmir knowing I was the one enjoying good fortune in this world. Faryal was pregnant again, and we announced the sex to the world in an original way when I punched a balloon full of confetti – the colour would reveal boy or girl. It was blue – Muhammad

Zaviyar was on his way, the perfect addition to our family. It was confirmation again that me and Faryal had something so, so good.

With Dib done, everything was full systems go for the Khan/Kell showdown. And then Covid happened. Boxing, like so many other sports, was stopped dead in its tracks. Football and cricket would eventually return behind closed doors. You couldn't do that with boxing. The glamour, the excitement, the entertainment is everything. For a fight, and a farewell, that should have been just around the corner I would have to wait thirty-two months.

If ever I needed another reminder that there's a lot more to life than boxing, Covid was it. For the first time in nearly twenty years I spent a prolonged period without training camps and fights getting in the way of normal life. Being stuck at home allowed me to build a bond with the kids, and Faryal too, in a way I'd never been able to before. It's no wonder that sportspeople so often end up divorced. For years, couples are virtual strangers. By the time a career comes to an end all that's left is a void. Covid allowed me a glimpse of how family life could be in retirement.

At the same time, I had to deal with the devastating news that Mum had been diagnosed with stage two pancreatic cancer. It seemed crazy to me that someone so strong could ever be felled by illness. She was the absolute rock around which everyone's world revolved. Thankfully, after months of anguish we were able to see our prayers had been answered and she was on the road to recovery. Even so, it was another moment to reassess. No one lasts for ever and time with loved ones is precious. Did I carry on cutting myself away from that environment? It seemed mad to do so.

As if I wasn't feeling disaffected enough with boxing, there was something else going on that made me feel increasingly queasy. Fights suddenly were as likely to feature a YouTuber as a boxer. When that kicked off I couldn't believe what I was seeing. I couldn't for the life of me understand why a professional boxer would get in the ring with a social influencer. I'd try to put myself in their boots. OK, there's a bit of a payday, but what happens if it all goes wrong and you end up getting beat? Potentially by someone who's never been to a training camp in their life? One lucky punch is all it takes and that's it, you're finished for good. All those years building your reputation – gone. And all because you've given in to some idiot goading you into the ring.

There's a flipside to that coin. A YouTuber could get badly hurt. That's what happens to people who don't know what they're doing. Boxing is the toughest sport in the world. Mess with it at your peril. But, as usual, it's money, not common sense, that talks.

After Covid, it would just get worse and worse. Boxers taking on mixed martial arts (MMA) fighters, strongmen having it out in the ring. It's like Covid changed everything – as if on the other side was a completely different world. People were no longer happy doing and seeing what they had before.

I made my name without social media. It didn't exist back then. I had to rely on magazines and newspapers to get my name out there. Now we've got fighters who think they're Charlie Big Bollocks before they've even done anything. They've got 100,000 followers on Instagram and think they're on top of the world. What they're really saying is they don't have the heart to reach the top the hard way, to build their reputation by fighting through the ranks. Basically they're lazy. They don't have the work ethic. They live off people blowing smoke up their arses. 'Superstars' without even winning a title. I had a different mentality. Forget numbers on social media, I was more worried about the numbers on my boxing record. There's no such thing as being a champion on social media. You can only be a champion in real life.

Beat Kell Brook in my final fight and, to my fans and to me, I'd be a champion one last time.

COACHING SESSION 10

My guess is that my honesty in this chapter will surprise a few people in and out of the sport. One thing someone like me is never supposed to admit is that they walked away from a challenge, even if it was one that was already lost.

It's only now that I feel ready to be totally honest about what happened at Madison Square Garden that night in April 2019. I could have carried on making out it was absolutely impossible for me to continue, but what really would be the point of doing that?

I reckon pretty much every person who reads this will have something in their past that didn't pan out quite how they've claimed down the years. I'll tell you now, it's a great feeling to get it off your chest.

As ever, it's fear of being judged that makes us hang on to stories that aren't quite true. If people want to judge me, fine. I'd just rather not carry baggage like that around any more.

ROUND ELEVEN

I had only one thought as I walked into the auditorium before the Kell Brook fight – *I DON'T WANT TO BE HERE*.

You'd think the big entrance, the noise, the music, the shouts, the cheers, the celebrity faces, the Manchester City and England footballer Jack Grealish and rock god Noel Gallagher among them, would have sparked something in me. But that jolt of electricity never appeared. As I turned the last concrete corner into a barrage of pyrotechnics and my entire team were ushered in a different direction, I felt empty inside.

Get in the ring, I thought, *get it done, and get out of here*.

If your heart isn't in a fight 100 per cent, then you're starting from a bad place.

If my motivation had been slipping away in the fights with Terence Crawford and Billy Dib, then by the time the Kell clash came round, after a two-year delay for Covid, it was on the floor. For two years I hadn't loved the sport. It just paid well. Without those big-money fights, I'd probably have ended up hating boxing. I'd have put so much into the sport only to end up not even having enough for myself, let alone those around me.

Everything just somehow felt different. The weigh-in, for example, made me feel nervous. I'd not done one for such a long time that it felt weirdly new to me. Normally, I'd not have batted an eyelid. A weigh-in was familiar territory to me. It was like I was being imprisoned by the sport whereas once it set me free.

Earlier, the pre-fight press conference had been similarly odd. While everyone else was fired up by the thought of this great long-awaited fight, I was just bored, running on automatic. I'd try to listen to what people were saying but their words were drowned out by the voice in my head – my voice – *I DON'T WANT TO DO THIS NO MORE.*

Don't get me wrong, on a basic level I did what was expected to sell the fight, and it worked – the clash was the hottest ticket in the country, selling out in seconds – but the words that came out of my mouth meant nothing. There were a few oohs and aahs when I told Kell I was going down a level to fight him, but it wasn't in any way said from the heart. My team had suggested I say it. I didn't believe it any more than they did. It was just a good line to help sell the fight. At that point, me and Kell were both prize fighters (those words again). When it's purely about ticket sales, bums on seats, that's what you have to do. It wasn't as if I didn't like Kell. I'd got no problem with him really. But do all the mouthing off beforehand

and that way it becomes a grudge match; a fight that everyone wants, and will pay, to see.

Like with Phil Lo Greco, there was one particular piece of pre-fight bullshit that did get me riled. Kell had been mouthing off that he was going to smash my 'poppadom chin'. As a British Pakistani, there was a racial element in the slur that got my back up, and I wasn't going to let him say crap like that without being challenged.

'That sounded racist to me,' I told him. 'Why did you say that?'

Kell came back with some lame excuse – 'Everyone knows they're very fragile, like your chin.' Normally, I would have wanted to lay out an opponent who said stuff like that, at the very least give them an unscheduled shower like Lo Greco, but in Kell's case I just felt sad. I'd never have had him down as someone who would say something like that. Why choose a word that related directly to my culture if that wasn't his intention? But then again pretty much anything goes in pre-fight talk. I've done it myself – said something daft and then later on thought *Shit! Did I really say that?*

More than anything I put Kell's attitude to me down to jealousy. We came through the ranks at round about the same time but he never had the fights I did, nor enjoyed the same kind of public acclaim. Put those two things together and he never made the same amount of money. That meant that, when it came to being on each other's radar, I was on his way more than he was on mine. For most of my career I never gave him a second thought.

He also held a grudge from the only other time we had stepped into the ring – a sparring session at an England training camp when we were both coming through as Olympic hopefuls in 2004. For years the way I'd told it was that there was only one winner that day; that despite him having more padding than a DFS sofa and me going about 50 per cent, pretty much one-handed, I'd given him a working over, and that was the end of his Athens hopes.

Kell never accepted what happened in those camps, and I don't blame him. In all honesty, that sparring session is so long in the past I've no idea what happened! I just gave my version of events to wind him up. Who were people going to believe? Me, who'd come back from the Olympics with a silver medal and gone on to be world champion? Or Kell, who'd not achieved half as much? Whatever happened, I never understood why he made it such a massive part of the story. To keep himself in the public eye? Maybe he couldn't stand the fact that, from Athens onwards, I got all the spotlight and not him.

In his view, I'd nicked his Olympic place, and that was the tale he stuck to down the years. The whole thing was crazy. I fought for that Olympic place. I gave up a lot, did it the hard way. Believe me, I didn't want to be locked away in training camps while my friends were out having fun, going on holiday or day trips. To get a place on the Olympic team you have to be a proven competitor, a winner. I wasn't hand-picked. No one said: 'Right, Amir Khan is going to earn more, get the recognition.' I was the best amateur and had proven it by becoming world junior champion earlier the same year. At that stage I'd done more than he could ever dream of. OK, he envied me but what was I supposed to do about it? That was his lookout. Truth is, I was a way better boxer than him and that's why I went to Athens. They could only send one lightweight. They knew I was a massive talent and I proved it by coming back with the silver medal, but Kell always thought he should have been picked over me. Even eighteen years on it was a great way to get under his skin.

With animosity swirling around us – again from him, not me – it was only natural that when we turned pro the rumour mill would start whirring. It seemed like every other week we were being lined up for a fight. As far as I was concerned it was just hot air. A fight with Kell didn't interest me. I had bigger fish to fry. I wanted to reach the top and Kell wasn't a rung on that ladder. I also saw my future long-term in America. Kell was stuck this side of the Atlantic. By the time I was beating the likes of Marcos

Maidana and was on top of the world, taking on Kell back in the UK would have been a backwards step.

Unlike him, I never needed that fight in my prime. Yes, it would have filled an arena, had a big audience in the UK, but that wasn't where I needed to be. That was a pity, but the point is that while he seemed obsessed, trying the usual verbal diarrhoea – 'Bambi on ice', for example, which must have taken a lot of thinking up – to get me to respond, he was invisible to me.

When our paths did cross, there was a decent chance of fireworks, which was no doubt on the mind of whoever invited us both on to Sky Sports' *Ringside* boxing show in 2012. They clearly knew sparks would fly. Even though Kell was nowhere near a target for me at that time you never miss a chance to put a potential opponent down. 'I used to box Kell all around the ring,' I said, giving Kell my best 'this will wind him up' smile. It did the job. He was fucked off big time.

By the time we did get in the ring ten years later, Kell had years of bitterness to feed off. We'd started off travelling on tracks side by side. Then he'd gone one way and I'd gone the other. Mine was the track to glory, his not so much. Not surprising that when the time came he wanted to beat me so badly. When someone has that much motivation to destroy another person, it doesn't matter who they are, they can do it. He'd have walked through a wall, he envied me that much. That was the big difference between us that night. He had that absolute desire whereas I was finished. I had no personal goals, but he really wanted my scalp. As ever, Kell needed me more than I needed him.

That's not to say I went into that fight expecting to lose. While I knew I wasn't the fighter I had been, I also knew that physically and mentally I was better than Kell. He was the same age as me but had been in more wars, suffered more wear and tear. If he'd been a car, he'd have been written off years ago. If he'd been younger than me, rather than finished, I would never have taken that fight. Instead I saw a fairly evenly matched clash that I could win.

I'd also done the preparation. I trained hard for that fight, harder than for any other, joining up with Brian 'BoMac' McIntyre, the perfect trainer for the job. His star man was Terence Crawford and together they knew everything there was to know about beating Kell — Crawford had put him on the floor and stopped him in four rounds just fifteen months previously.

My own fight with Crawford might have ended in controversy, and BoMac hadn't held back about me not coming out of my corner after his fighter's low blow, but there was no beef from any of us when we were reunited. I had no problem in recognising that Crawford was the superior boxer, same as I'd had plenty of time to reflect on how well they'd worked me out before that night in Madison Square Garden. Point was, they had clearly done exactly the same with Kell, and now they could pass that knowledge on to me as we set up camps, first in Crawford's home town of Omaha, Nebraska, and then in the ridiculous chill of Colorado Springs.

Omaha was perfect preparation, so quiet compared to big city life and a place where mentally I could reset and try to prepare for what was to come. But it was on the way there from New York that something bad happened. As we taxied towards the runway, me and a friend, also Asian, were confronted in our front-row seats by airline staff. From the minute we'd sat down I'd noticed them looking us up and down suspiciously but, as usual on a flight, I'd fallen asleep almost straight away. I woke a few minutes later surrounded by aircrew.

I heard a woman's voice. 'Can you please stand up?'

'I'm sorry, what?' I was still half asleep.

'We need to remove you from the plane.'

Pandemic restrictions were still in place and they were making a big thing about my friend's face covering not being pulled up high enough.

I protested – 'No. No. This can't be right.'

By now, the plane was returning to the gate. They really were going to kick us off. Next thing we knew there were five cops coming on board. We grabbed our stuff and that was that. I really didn't want to make a scene with half the plane staring at us.

Back in the terminal, a couple of the cops realised who I was. They were really apologetic, and said they could see we weren't causing a problem, but pointed out that if the airline staff wanted us off they had no choice but to act. No charges were issued and we reasoned we'd get a later flight – except, as we soon found out, the airline had banned us. Nebraska isn't a particularly common destination and we'd have to wait forty-eight hours until we could fly with another carrier.

For me, we'd been victims of blatant racism. Would they have had two white people removed for something so trivial? I doubt it. There is still suspicion of Asian people travelling by air in America. A few years earlier, I'd been due to travel to the US on the anniversary of 9/11 to commentate on a fight when I was told my visa had been refused and I couldn't get on the plane. Thankfully, I was still friends with David Cameron, now the PM, after he'd come to visit my gym a few years earlier. I rang his office and filled them in on what had happened. A few minutes later they called me back – 'Don't worry, it's sorted.' Since 9/11 and also the 7/7 bombings in London I have done nothing but try to unite people, but sometimes that kind of thing, that understanding, falls on deaf ears. It wasn't the perfect start to the fight journey and, as time would tell, it wouldn't be the perfect end either.

Funnily enough, once I started training in Colorado Springs, I began to wish I could get chucked off the plane to camp more often! I'm sure the Rocky Mountains is a very beautiful place but as I ran its paths and trails the only thing I saw was my frozen breath, each thin lungful gulped in as the 7,000ft altitude drained my energy away.

There are black bears in the Rockies. They say if you see one you should stand as still as you can, don't make a move. I was one of the few people up there hoping to meet one. A wrestle might have warmed me up a bit. It wasn't much fun – super cold, like minus six. By far the coldest of any place I'd ever been to train. As I toiled up those trails, in all honesty all that was keeping me going was the thought of the payday, and the knowledge that the heating would be on in the gym.

To be fair, BoMac had never given me the impression any of this was going to be easy. On an initial, getting-to-know-each-other visit he'd sprung a surprise sparring session on me. Next thing I knew, the gloves were being laced up and a crowd was gathering – big guys who clearly hadn't come to see a bit of gentle jabbing. It was like having a fight on the street – I had no choice but to go with it. Step away and I'd have been called a pussy. This was no quick in-and-out either. Two fighters had been lined up. I had to keep going while they rotated.

It was hard, really hard, but actually I was always in control. Everyone saw I'd still got it, including me. Remember, this was a stage when my mind was full of doubt. Age and injury weren't on my side. BoMac was clever – he'd set the session up not to shock me but to reassure me. I might not have been full of motivation but at least I knew that, as a boxer, I had what was needed.

From then on, it was all systems go, the camp itself split between Omaha and the nightmare peaks of Colorado where, as well as runs, I'd spar, each four-minute round worth eight at ground level.

Crawford himself would check my progress. One of the pound-for-pound greats, he'd even get into the ring to work the pads. Imagine that – like Ronaldo carrying the kitbag. Some boxers might take exception to being schooled by a fellow pro. I wasn't one of them. Crawford could be tough in the gym – every time I thought a session was over there'd be another push-up to do, another gym machine to climb aboard – but he was an all-time icon.

You'd have to be mad not to hang on his every word. I knew from experience how being around great fighters can only make you better – training with multiple world champions Andre Ward and Manny Pacquiao had shown me exactly that – and now I was getting even more. Everything was hands-on with Crawford and BoMac. I had a team who were 100 per cent invested in me and I felt like a kid again. For a while my motivation changed. I wanted to show Kell how good I was, that I wasn't a done fighter. I wanted to prove a point to him. That's what made me train hard for that fight. I pushed myself as hard as I could – and then the full-on regime began to take its toll.

I hadn't realised it, but actually I was overtraining. I'd wake up in the morning like a dead man. My back hurt, my legs, hips, arms, knees. I'd never trained so hard for so long in my life, and this after I'd been out of the ring for more than eighteen months, Covid making anything else an impossibility. I was getting more stiffness, more lactic acid build-up, and I'd also torn a shoulder ligament.

You might wonder why I didn't speak up, but in all honesty I was too scared. Once you've committed to a trainer you have to go with it. For that period of time, they know best. Also, I knew exactly how it would look. The minute you start talking about niggles and injuries, people automatically think you're coming up with excuses, preparing the ground for slacking off in training or not performing in the ring. I'm a proud man and that was the last image I wanted to project.

While my body changed, sometimes for better but

usually for worse, my original mentality returned. While BoMac was an amazing coach, and he paired me with some great sparring partners, no matter how hard I tried, mentally I couldn't feel the buzz. I thought back to my fight against Marco Antonio Barrera. At that point I was twenty-two years old, fighting a man of thirty-five. I remembered how old Barrera seemed to me, almost as if he was from another time. And now that was me. I compared my mindset then to my mindset now. Compared that version of me, the young lad anxious to make it as a pro, desperate to leap forward and take the biggest fights, to the prize fighter I was now. Just miles apart. Fighting for totally different reasons. I'd fallen out of love with boxing and running around those freezing mountain tracks wasn't going to miraculously bring it back.

As I ran, I thought again of what I'd seen at the Boxing Hall of Fame – fighters who were broke, no money and now their pride, and in some cases sanity, was slipping away too. When you're in a blood sport like boxing, you never ever want to be in that position. In my head, I was always going to win that fight against Kell, but if, God forbid, it went wrong, I knew I was getting security. The way I looked at it, I'd rather suffer and make an eight-figure fee than make the same amount from four or five smaller fights. When you've got almost $10 million on the table, you're not going to turn that down. You may think that's cynical. I didn't. At the end of the day, that was my kids' money and I'd worked hard for it. I don't care what they do, no sportsperson deserves to earn more than boxers. We literally put our lives on the line. Disrespect our sport and it bites back big time. In boxing, it only takes a nanosecond for everything you've fought for to disappear. You can be brain-damaged. You can even end up dead. You are only ever one punch away from disaster. That is a fact. Anyone who says boxing is easy needs to spend twenty-four hours in a fighter's shoes.

There was something else that nagged at me. If I didn't do the fight, people would always hate me for it. To the end it was important for me to be the people's champion, and turning away from that fight would have massively jeopardised that status. The whole country and beyond wanted to see that battle, this 'feud', come to a head. It had been talked about for so long, how could I refuse? Mentally and physically I was nowhere near where I needed to be, but I had to give it to the fans, and to Kell.

· · ·

The fight might actually have happened earlier. In 2017, Kell was the IBF welterweight champion, so for once it did actually make sense that we should meet up. Money proved the problem. To my mind, and to any sane person,

I was the bigger name of the two. I had achieved ten times more than Kell, but I was meant to split the purse down the middle. Any boxer will tell you that's a shit deal. I wanted the larger share. I hadn't fought professionally for thirteen years to sell myself down the river to massage his ego. At that point Kell and his promoter, Eddie Hearn, walked away. Kell took on Errol Spence Jr and lost. Great decision on his part. Although chances are that, at that point, he'd have lost to me too.

A few months later I actually signed with Eddie Hearn's Matchroom stable, a surprise to many because me and Eddie had never really got on. That particular spat dated back to my fight with Paul McCloskey. At the press conference I could hear this bloke moaning about the fight being shown on Primetime instead of the bigger audience of Sky. I was with Golden Boy at the time and he was having a go at Oscar De La Hoya, asking him what he knew about boxing.

'What do I know about boxing?' Oscar replied. Everyone started laughing. Bear in mind that he'd won eleven world titles in his time.

I remember asking someone: 'Who the hell is this guy?'

'Eddie Hearn – Barry Hearn's son,' they replied.

No two ways about it, Eddie made a fool of himself at that press conference. I beat McCloskey and after that he never stopped having a go at me. He had Kell Brook and he wanted me to fight him. He was forever having a pop at me on social media. Face to face he'd have shit himself, but Eddie was a proper keyboard warrior, happy to say something on Twitter or to a camera but never to your face.

When I was at Matchroom, everyone assumed that would be it – Kell and me were bound to end up in the ring together. But still for me it wasn't the mega-fight that it would have been for Kell. Terence Crawford in front of a packed Madison Square Garden was what appealed to me. Only in Kell World was he number one choice.

The irony is that by the time the fight, which he'd built up for years and years, finally happened, Eddie wasn't actually the promoter. In the end Kell had split from Eddie, claiming he was too busy with his other fighters to look after him, and Matchroom was behind me too. It was Ben Shalom, of promotional company BOXXER, who finally got the deal over the line.

Kell wasn't slow in celebrating the prospect. 'I really dislike the man and I really can't wait to punch his face in,' he said. 'I can't wait to get my knuckles to the nearest point of the gloves and drill it straight into his face.'

As it turned out his comment about the gloves might well have come back to haunt him. On the night, Kell was wearing horsehair gloves, much firmer than foam gloves, and a big weapon for power hitters like him. Horsehair gloves are bad news for the head of anyone who gets in the way of them. I'd go so far as to say that potentially they are killers, to the extent they have at times been banned. The fight contract specifically spelled out that horsehair gloves weren't to be worn but my suspicions had been raised at the weigh-in. I'd seen Kell's gloves and to a trained eye like mine they didn't look like foam. On the night of the fight I wanted to see the gloves he was using but Kell's team wouldn't let anyone into his changing room.

By now, with the fight in danger, things were heating up. The British Boxing Board of Control (BBBC) general secretary, Robert Smith, said that if the bout was delayed or called off my team would be given a massive fine. I wasn't having it.

'Look,' I told him, 'I've had forty pro fights. I know when a pair of gloves aren't foam. You have to inspect them.'

'No, no, no.'

My dad was insistent. 'OK – we don't see the gloves, we don't fight.' He wasn't bluffing. We would 100 per cent have walked.

This wasn't us being awkward. If I went out in foam gloves and him in horsehair it could never be a fair fight.

He could hit me ten times as hard. He could hurt me, do serious damage.

Eventually, as the minutes counted down, someone managed to get hold of a glove like Kell's. He took a knife to it and ripped it open. Guess what? Horsehair everywhere. That's why, if you watch footage of the fight, you see Kell Brook changing his gloves in the ring – something that never ever happens.

Smith was embarrassed but, as the person who would have felt the full force of those gloves, I wasn't going to let it drop that easily. To the millions at home, I knew how it would look – that I was making excuses, trying to get out of the fight.

'You are the head of boxing in this country,' I pointed out. 'I told you what was going on and you wouldn't listen.' He apologised and walked away. Forget how the fight panned out, I could have made a much bigger deal about that incident. The BBBC were lucky I didn't.

• • •

The fight itself would go the way I feared. The shoulder issue meant that in a battle where I needed 120 per cent I had only 70. The inability to raise my right arm properly meant I was severely restricted in my shots. Look at the video and you can clearly see the red circular mark from the cupping – using a sealed cup to draw a small area of the body upwards to help aid soft tissue recovery – the physio had performed the night before. It helped a little, but as I hit the pads, trying to get in the zone before the fight, I knew it was nowhere near enough.

The omens were bad from the start. Leaving the hotel, my car pulled away before Faryal had a chance to say goodbye. That's a big moment for any fighter's partner. The odds may be tiny, but there's always a chance that the person they love might suffer a life-changing injury, or worse. Imagine how that feels. Faryal is a bag of nerves at fight times. She would never go to the arena and would literally turn her phone off during the fight itself. Instead that time was spent in prayer.

In the case of the Kell Brook fight, she'd definitely not have liked what she was seeing. I couldn't get into the gears, again couldn't find the reach. For every blow I landed, Kell landed two. In the fifth round, seeing that I was weakening, he stepped up the assault. A few minutes later, in the sixth, as the ropes propped me up, he caught me with a vicious uppercut. The ref had seen enough. In he stepped and stopped it. My protests fell on deaf ears, but in all honesty I knew it was over anyway. For me, the fight, and boxing. As Kell punched the air, all I wanted to do was get to Faryal, climb on a flight, and go home to my kids. The pyrotechnics were going off no more.

At the after-fight press conference me and Kell wrapped our arms around each other, a forging of a mutual respect that had otherwise been lacking, something which often happens when two 'sworn enemies' finally get in the ring together. For both of us there was relief that this most long-running of boxing soap operas had finally come to an end.

I couldn't have been more impressed with how Kell handled himself. I know for sure that if it had been me in his boots I'd have been absolutely flying, but actually in the hours, and even days, that followed he was very quiet. He never waved that victory in my face. Maybe Kell knew in himself that this wasn't the real Amir Khan he was fighting. Whatever, in the time since, I've messaged him to say it would be nice to have coffee one day and talk as men rather than boxers.

If anything, I feel sorry for Kell. I still get the same amount of love as I did before that fight. People still want to stop me in the street, talk to me about my career, have a photo with me – and I'm very grateful for that. I'm respected for stepping into that ring even though I was nowhere near the boxer I was, had nothing to win – I'd already proved myself a great – and a lot more to lose. But did anything really change for Kell? He's not done much since and nobody really cares about him. Even though he beat me, he doesn't have the same following on social media or get calls to go on TV shows. That's sad, because Kell is a great boxer, but on the other hand you have to build your audience. I did exactly that by taking on big fights throughout my career. Take on the big fights and the more chance you'll be involved in the epic battles that people remember – and be remembered yourself.

While Kell's behaviour was exemplary and dignified, there's always others happy to put the boot in. I get there'll always be people on social media ready to slag you off. They either forget or don't understand what it takes to get this far in boxing. They see you in a nice house with a nice car and think you've got lazy; that it comes easy. What they don't see is the hard graft that it's built on. If becoming a successful boxer is so easy, how come everyone doesn't do it? Maybe it's because most jobs don't involve someone trying to knock your lights out.

What really gets me is when fellow fighters either start or join in the pile-on. Carl Froch is the perfect example. I've never ever said anything bad about Carl but he's never been able to keep his mouth shut about me, always putting me down. I think that's envy – envy that he didn't make the kind of money I did. He hates me for that. It's like when my name's mentioned he takes it personally. And there he was, at it again after the Kell fight, calling me 'Bambi Khan' and crowing about how much he'd enjoyed watching the 'beatdown'.

Carl's comments don't get to me. He does it to lots of people. Presumably it makes him happy to sit there in retirement spouting off and he sees it as an OK way to make a living, although I think most people in the sport consider that kind of behaviour pretty average. I've generally bit my tongue about Carl but Faryal is a different person to me. 'I rarely ever say bad about anyone,' she tweeted after his last outburst, 'but I actually can't stand Carl Froch. Simply rude and annoying. Wonder if it upsets him that Khan made more money than him.' You just don't mess with Faryal!

I actually look back at the Kell fight with pride. Nothing in life comes easy, and the financial reward I received certainly didn't (I did treat myself to a Lamborghini sports car to lessen the blow!). More than any monetary reward, it made me feel good to know that every person in that arena was on the edge of their seat – that for one last time I was generating that electricity, that buzz of excitement, a voltage surging through every row.

That's the type of person I've always been. As much as I was a quality boxer, people also invested in the personality I showed in the ring. If they'd thought I was bland or boring, they'd never have bought into me in the way they did. People didn't know what to expect from me, and they liked that. I lived on the edge. I was always willing to go the extra mile to fulfil whatever might be waiting for me. I wanted, more than anything, to entertain.

After twenty years at the top, I might have grown weary of boxing, but that doesn't mean I'm not proud of what I achieved. I took on the biggest fights and went out there all guns blazing. I don't care if people want to call me too offensive. I wanted my fights to be as exciting as the ones that had excited me as a kid. Just like I used to sit watching the big fights on TV, fantasising about being champion of the world, maybe now I'll be the fighter who a kid watches on YouTube and thinks *I want to be like him*. I hope that happens. It's amazing to think you could be the person who puts the fire in someone's belly. That's proper shiver-up-the-spine stuff.

There was a rematch clause with Kell, but I didn't want to do it. For me, the whole Kell thing was done with. People never believe it when you say stuff like this, but even if I'd beaten Kell I would still have quit. I'd done everything I wanted in the sport. The Kell fight was the full stop. And in front of 20,000 people in what is pretty much my home town in Manchester it was a good full stop, one that emphasised the attitude that embodied my career – a fighter who never shied away.

I treated my boxing career as an adventure and I'm glad I could take so many people along for the ride. It was one hell of a journey, a rollercoaster I could never get off. Boxing is an addiction. As soon as one fight finishes you want to do it again. But not this time.

I walked through the door into our house in Dubai, let my bag drop to the floor and was swamped by Lamaisah, Alayna and Zaviyar. They kissed me and held me and I wondered if they could see my bruises.

COACHING SESSION II

Boxing is strange. Before a fight it is full of hate. Afterwards, suddenly fighters can be honest with each other and often find they actually get on. Let's face it, we've got a lot in common. We're often from quite similar backgrounds and we've chosen to make a living out of the most brutal sport in the world.

There's a lesson to be learned there. The person you consider your enemy very often isn't. They're a lot more like you than you think. There's a lot more satisfaction in finding friendship against the odds than there is in keeping up some silly feud. I can honestly say that some of my best friends are people who've once tried to take my head off!

I'm not sure me and Kell will ever go on holiday together but if we get stuck in a lift I think we'll be OK. I like that. Long-term grudges are a waste of energy. They're destructive, stop you thinking straight and stop you moving on.

Remove them from your life and you will feel a thousand times better.

ROUND TWELVE

I thought Kell Brook would be the last battle of my life. Instead I ended up facing the biggest fight of them all. For my reputation.

On the night of the fight I gave a specimen of urine for the testers from UK Anti-Doping. Nothing unusual about that. Drug testing isn't just what I wanted to do, it was something, unlike some other boxers, I insisted on. Prior to the fight I'd been tested three times. Everything was clear. I heard a few weeks later that this time they found the prohibited substance ostarine, used to build muscle mass, in my urine. The amount was equivalent to a grain of salt in a swimming pool.

If the drug had been detected sooner, in the early days of the training camp, for example, people might have been justified in thinking I had been using it to put muscle on. But now? On the night? It made no sense. In the run-up to that fight I was doing all I could to make the weight. I had to lose ten pounds. It had been agreed by both fighters that for every pound we were over the agreed weight we would lose a six-figure sum. How stupid would it have been for me to put muscle on at that time?

Everything I put in my body for weeks before that

fight was monitored. I had a nutritionist, a cook and a dietician who did everything for me. The cook would prepare my food in isolation to prevent any risk of it being contaminated. I could only think the ostarine had come from maybe sharing a drink or shaking someone's hand and it then being transferred to my mouth. At the end of the day, the fighter is responsible for what's in their body. Because of that, all I could argue was unintentional use.

I was called before an independent tribunal to give evidence. They ruled out 'deliberate or reckless conduct', and agreed the use was unintentional, but under the strict liability rule I would be subjected to a two-year ban. Because the ruling wasn't revealed until April 2023, and the test was in February 2022, by the time the announcement came I had already served more than a year of the penalty.

That was little consolation. The damage was done. All I could think about was what the headlines would look like in the papers. As a 100 per cent clean fighter, I hated the thought of what would be said about me – 'he'll have been doing it all his career'. To be associated with drugs is the last thing I ever wanted, and now the label is attached to me for ever.

It upsets me massively that all my life I've never ever taken anything and now people will stop believing me. Never in a million years would I do something like that.

I've always been a clean fighter — always talked about being a clean fighter. Remember, I was on the wrong end of a boxer on drugs when I fought Lamont Peterson. I was on such a downer after that fight. I'd worked so hard, done so much, and then been 'beaten' by someone who was basically supercharged. Why would I ever jeopardise my own reputation after seeing that up close? Since that fight I asked to be blood and urine tested on each and every occasion. I was so anti-drugs that I was the one constantly calling UK Anti-Doping (UKAD) during training for the Kell Brook fight asking where they were and why they hadn't been testing. And it was me also who insisted on testing being in the contract.

Right back to my Olympics days, being drug tested has been part of my job. I can be tested any place, any time. Testers have come out to Dubai, to the Philippines, wherever I've been based or training. I have to give my whereabouts on an app so the testers always know where I am. I've had knocks on the door so early in the morning I've still been in bed. Why would I jeopardise a clean reputation built up over twenty years for the last fight of my career? The testers themselves have said the amount of ostarine in my urine would never have done anything anyway. It wasn't like I went in there all guns blazing. I looked flat in that fight because I felt flat. Like I said, it was a fight I had no passion for. In my head, as a boxer, I was done. None of it makes any sense, but it's a burden I now carry.

Meanwhile, the fight game goes on. It's a sport where, no matter how long you've been retired, how many times you say you're done, there's always someone trying to persuade you to do one more dance. Boxing is the biggest comeback sport going and so nobody ever truly believes you've gone. Even after the announcement that it was the end of the road I had guys come up to me in the street – 'Amir, come on, are you really retired?'

'Yeah, 100 per cent.'

It was coming straight from the horse's mouth and still they didn't believe it. The media was the same. Constant conversations. And I get why. In fighting sports especially, when someone says they're retired, they're not really. They're just biding their time before the offer they can't refuse comes in and they're back in that ring giving it another go. For any prize fighter, if the price or the opposition is right, there will always be that temptation to lace the gloves up one more time.

But the fact is I've achieved pretty much everything I want to in the ring. And who knows, the next fight might be the one where, finally, it all goes horribly wrong. The one where you get seriously hurt. Any boxer, even the very best, is only one punch away from oblivion and, the longer you go on, the more your reflexes are compromised, the more your muscle memory vanishes, and the more likely it is to happen. The boxer who says that doesn't worry them isn't telling the truth. I'd always planned to retire at thirty, and that was a good plan because, as it turned out, that was pretty much when my ability really started to decline. By the time I quit I was already five years over that limit – I had already taken risks with my health. Turning my back on that life wasn't an issue. I knew it was the right thing to do. I could genuinely say I had taken the biggest fights open to me. My challenge was to find other adventures.

• • •

Because I've always defined myself as a boxer, people wonder if it's been hard to switch to a different mindset. After all, professional sport is littered with those who have found the return to 'civvy street' to be a testing, if not impossible, challenge. Endlessly, they try to get back into boxing because it's all they know.

For me, though, it's different. I'll be straight – to step away from boxing has actually been a relief. I know that's a strange thing to say but truth is, as a top-level pro, boxing dominates every minute of every day. It's all you and the people around you talk about. Even when the talking stops you can't escape the nagging thoughts that burrow slowly from the back to the front of your mind. 'I need to go to the gym and train. Who's going to be my next opponent? Is it the right fight? What do I need to do to beat him? When am I going to get a date? Do I need to go to America for a training camp?' There's no 'off' button. This stuff is going round your head on a loop. Forget the actual physical work that being a professional boxer entails, this endless internal chatter is in itself totally exhausting. Imagine the relief when that's gone. When I made the decision to retire, the first thing I thought was I'm not going to have to think about any of that stuff any more. It was a massive weight off my shoulders. For the first time in my life I could finally relax.

Don't get me wrong, I will always be massively proud of my career, but equally I'm totally comfortable with being able to say I'm glad it's over. I'd committed so much to boxing and I just couldn't do it any more. I've always had a young outlook on life – I don't want to grow up, don't feel like I ever have, and am quite happy with that – but in those later years I felt like the old man I used to tell my friends they were turning into. My back would hurt if I sat down for too long – aches and pains everywhere. I'd lost the love for the sport.

I know this doesn't sound great but, to be perfectly honest, by the end I was sick of it. I'd put the best part of a quarter of a century into boxing and that was enough. Inevitably, after a while, you begin to ask: 'Why am I still doing this? Do I really still need it, want it, as badly as I did before?' And if the answers are negative then maybe it's time to turn away. There's only so much you can do in life and quitting when I did meant I was young enough to start again elsewhere.

As someone who has never liked sitting around doing nothing, I was lucky that, towards the end of my career, plans were beginning to form in a different direction to boxing. I might not have covered myself in glory the last time I was on reality TV – I've never had a guilt-free bowl of strawberries and cream since – but there had been talk for a while of taking myself and Faryal's relationship, the whole craziness of our life together, and turning it into a TV show.

The publicity surrounding our 'split' a few years previously might, for once, actually have worked in our favour. There was clearly a lot of interest in this marriage of British and American Asians, the glamorous intelligent influencer New Yorker and the down-to-earth boxer from the working-class Lancashire town of Bolton. From the outside you could see why a TV show might work – there was a lot to compare and contrast!

As I mentioned, Jonathan Ross had seized on just that culture gap when, during an appearance on his chat show, he put up pictures of Times Square and Bolton bus station! I get it. To a lot of people we must look like a bit of an odd couple, but actually underneath we work pretty well together. OK, there's always a few flare-ups along the way, but that's our personalities. I've never been one to hold back in terms of showing who I am – never have, never will – and Faryal is the same, although in a slightly different, more measured way. She's very strong-minded, determined. She's never going to sit back and just let life happen – she's in it all the way. She's also very honest.

I've got a few marks here and there but I'm lucky – I'm the only fighter who's taken a few punches to the face and it's made me look better! Keeping my weight down over the years has certainly helped my long-term health. However, Faryal doesn't hold back. She keeps telling me: 'When you put weight on you don't look your best.' I have to keep on my toes otherwise she gives it to me good.

The BBC approached us with the idea for a show called *Meet the Khans: Big in Bolton* – 'World boxing champion Amir Khan and influencer wife Faryal open the doors to their crazy, fabulous family life in their beloved Bolton and dazzling Dubai.' That basic description was true but, once the show was broadcast, a lot of its popularity was a fascination with how on earth two people, on the outside so different, manage to live together and make it work. Watch *Meet the Khans* for half an hour and you'd probably conclude that me and Faryal are on the brink. I was going to say that's not true – but actually we probably have been on the brink for a very long time!

We stay strong for the kids. They bring us together because we both want them to grow up with two parents. I think a lot of parents are like that – they neglect their own future for the happiness of their children. We'd both admit our marriage has never been easy. As we've grown older, we've realised we are two very different people. We see things and react in different ways. I'm generally a straight talker – if I don't like something, I'll say so. But there are times when I'll let it build and build. We both have that side to us, where we'll sit and stew on a problem rather than talk about it – and so often that's where the problems start.

It's no secret, as this book has shown, that me and Faryal have had our ups and downs, and I don't think it hurts to bring in that element of reality. It helps build a connection with the audience – our lives aren't just glitz and glamour, we have problems just like everyone else. The thing with reality TV though is the makers build it into a storyline – *What's going to happen next? Tune in next week to find out!* – and it's weird sometimes to think of yourself in that position. I'm not saying what you see on screen isn't true – it is – but it does sometimes feel like you're living an imagined version of your life.

If anything, though, *Meet the Khans* has been good for our relationship. The show is very much about us both and so forces us together a lot of the time. Good thing really. If I worked alone on the programme, away for long periods, she'd be thinking: *What the hell? He's having a holiday!* Because it's the two of us, she can see it's work as well. The producers could clearly see the benefits of it being a joint enterprise. Put me and Faryal in the same room and nine times out of ten the result will be a mix of fun and fireworks. Faryal's not averse to the odd prank either. She once told me she'd lost £2 million in a banking error. She put my reaction up on YouTube. It wasn't pretty! Well, how would you react if someone told you they'd just accidentally dumped two million quid down the drain?

We also try honestly to reveal the stress of family life with small kids and, as I'm sure many viewers recognise, what a strain on a relationship that can be. Any prospective parents out there certainly get a full-on idea of what family life just might be like, especially with a good cop (me), bad cop (Faryal) approach that causes so much grief! The hardest part of *Meet the Khans* is undoubtedly that it takes us away from our beautiful children from time to time. When that happens, we make sure we speak to Lamaisah, Alayna and Zaviyar three times a day to make sure they're OK. Even so, I know it must be hard for them. They miss us so much when we're not there. I have to say to them: 'Mummy and Daddy have to go work so we can earn money for us to enjoy a good life, to have nice things.' We're lucky that they have such loving nannies who put their heart and soul into looking after them.

For boxing fans, *Meet the Khans* has also shown the reality of life in the run-up to a big fight – the entire second season followed the battle with Kell – but the real beauty of the programme is that it's taken me away from pure boxing fans and into a whole new audience where I'm as likely to get stopped in the street by someone's grandma asking me about Faryal as I am by someone reminding me of a great victory or – which does happen sometimes! – when I was laid out on the floor.

I find it odd to be labelled a reality TV star when I've always thought of myself as a boxer, but I know as well that it's good not to be forever trapped in your past. Since *Meet the Khans*, I've had people come up to me – 'Oh my god, I can't believe how chilled out you are. You come across so different.' And I have to remind them: 'This is me – all that was for boxing. For TV.' At a press conference you've got somebody who wants to knock your head off – you're not going to be nice to him. It's all part of the game to come across as confident, cocky. That meant that people who saw me only as a boxer never saw the real side of me; that it was an act put on for boxing.

There's an actor in all boxers. There has to be. Mike Tyson comes across as this really dangerous guy, a pit bull, when actually he's one of the most soft-hearted people I've ever met. I've had him crying next to me as he's telling me stories. What you see is an act, a drama, a soap opera created to make money. Imagine if boxers were like they are at press conferences all the time – they'd be burnt out in twelve months. It would be exhausting, so we have to adopt different characters. Depending on the fight, sometimes it's your place to be the one everyone loves, who they want to see swing that knockout punch. Other times, you're the baddie, the one they all hate. They can't wait to see you laid out on the canvas. One of the big reasons I wanted to do the programme was to close the door on all that and show the real me.

That includes talking about mental health, a subject that, as someone who had his own struggle when my world fell apart back in 2017, is so important to me. I don't think it hurts on a national TV channel to show a boxer, the classic alpha male, being honest about how he feels on the inside; how he is navigating that switch back to civvy street that I know can be so hard mentally for a lot of sportspeople.

Signing up for *Meet the Khans* before the end of my career gave me an idea of how retirement could be. Quitting is a dangerous time for any boxer and maybe if I wasn't so busy with the show and a million other commitments then walking away from the sport would have hit me harder. If there was nothing for me beyond boxing I'd have probably done what a lot of other fighters do and tried to stay in the game a little bit longer. Considering my love for the sport at this point was non-existent, and my physical condition was definitely not what it had been, that would have been a catastrophic idea.

The life I was building outside the ring ultimately helped me to walk away with hope and confidence, whereas a lot of sportspeople find themselves totally lost. You see it with football. The final whistle blows and players are destined to spend the rest of their days gambling, drinking too much, trying to find the same buzz at the bottom of a beer glass or vodka bottle. No way was I going to be in that club. I wanted to make sure that if I was going to retire, I could fall back on something else.

• • •

I'd already half-built another life for myself. While some boxers turned up, did the fight, and then disappeared until the next time, I was much more in the media. During the 2018 World Cup, *Good Morning Britain* introduced a *Good Evening Britain* show to talk about the latest events at the tournament in Russia. I found myself on a panel with Jeremy Corbyn, Danny Dyer – and Pamela Anderson!

Piers Morgan, the presenter, obviously wanted something beyond a boring old football show, which is what he got. Danny and Jeremy were more keen to talk about politics than football, while Pamela, who I think had been booked because she was dating a French footballer at the time, didn't have a clue about England's or anyone else's chances. I was sat there wondering what on earth I'd let myself in for. Earlier in my career, meanwhile, I'd made a programme for Channel 4 called *Amir Khan's Angry Young Men*, where I mentored a bunch of lads from difficult backgrounds and showed them how boxing could help them find a better way in life.

Often I'd turn up on TV shows that had nothing to do with sport – not many people realise I once picked the numbers on *Countdown*! I was also getting into punditry and commentating. I wouldn't have done any of that if I hadn't enjoyed it, but I knew also that I was building a platform for the day I stopped boxing. I was always scared of having nothing to do. I didn't honestly think that would happen, but who knows? I've seen fighters I loved, who did really well in the sport, and then as soon as they retired the doors shut. I wanted to make sure those doors didn't close on me.

If anything, during the later years of my career, I had too much going on. I was acting like there were forty-eight hours in a day. In all honesty, I'm still working out that work–life balance. I'm busier now than I ever was as a boxer. I can do anything, whereas before I had to turn so much down – 'Sorry, guys, I'm away at training camp.' I couldn't commit to something a couple of months down the line because chances were my boxing would get in the way.

Every day is a busy day. If it's not sorting out the wedding hall development, it's sticking the kit back on and having my boxing movements digitally recorded for a video game. If it's not a breakfast meeting to discuss crisis reaction in Pakistan, it's a late-night call for an interview in LA. The retirement Amir is the same as the fighter Amir – all in or not in at all.

As a fighter, you learn quickly. Compromise your training, your preparation, your mentality, and you pay a very heavy price. So that's the way I see life now. I don't do anything half-heartedly; I do everything properly. I suppose in some ways I've gone from being competitive against an opponent to being competitive against myself. If that means I'll get to bed at two in the morning and be up again at five to get a project over the line, then fine.

Meet the Khans also keeps me busy. It's more work than people think. Long, long days filming. Everything in TV seems to take for ever, especially when you're from a sport that can be over in seconds. Compared to boxing, TV is like cricket – the slowest Test match dragged out for five days. I spend half the time trying not to fall asleep. While I have the odd moan, I do of course genuinely love the show. It takes me to places, makes me meet people, that otherwise I'd never have known.

I'm constantly being asked to do all sorts of programmes, some which make more sense than others. I was recently asked to do *Celebrity MasterChef*, which I expect will give a few laughs to anyone who saw my microwaved scrambled eggs on *Meet the Khans*. *Strictly Come Dancing* has also been mentioned, although I'm terrible at dancing and would spend most of my time apologising to whichever poor professional was given the job of training me.

Back in the real world, eventually I'd like to be a property entrepreneur – one who doesn't make the same mistake as the wedding hall. This time I'll buy something ready! People say I'm too honest to operate in the business world, and that there are sharks out there who'll take advantage, but I'll never change. I've done OK in boxing by being myself – why should I throw that out the window now? This is me. This is the way I am. In sport, I saw a lot of bullshitting. I've experienced it and I've learned from it. Avoid the bullshit and you don't end up in a mess. If you don't like something, it's best to stay quiet or walk away.

At the same time as forging a new life, I don't want to do too much too quickly. I want to enjoy my retirement. I've been non-stop busy since I came back from the Olympics in 2004. I'd quite like the chance to get a bit bored first!

Thankfully, I have Dubai as a bolthole. I love the sense of relaxation it gives me. No one can get hold of me there, whereas in Bolton if someone wants to meet me, or talk over an idea, I can't say no. I'm really not very good at saying no! I'm one of those people who think everything's only going to take twenty minutes – and three hours later I'm still there!

Dubai is a battery recharge. That's why, when I come back to the UK, I work like a dog. I'm busy every minute of every day. And that's how I like it. What's the point of me putting my feet up? I can do that over there. By the time I get on that plane back to the UAE I feel like I'm way past my sell-by date. I hear people say: 'Amir's made his money and now he's dropped the UK like a stone,' but they couldn't be more wrong. I go there for my health and my mindset, to get away from everything when sometimes it just gets too much.

. . .

There's another reason Dubai appeals to me – safety. My whole view of the UK changed one day in April 2022 when I walked out of an east London restaurant with Faryal. I crossed the road to our car with her a little way behind.

The whole thing came out of nowhere. I knew a lot of people in east London, so someone running up to me wasn't necessarily a sign of danger. But then, before I knew it, I was being pushed against a car – looking down the barrel of a gun. I was confused, shocked. Part of me actually wondered if it was a friend playing a stupid trick on me. It wasn't.

Aside from on the police in Pakistan I've never seen a gun in my life. It's just not something you expect to see in England. Carrying a gun in England is serious shit. These thoughts were going through my head without me even realising it. I looked at the mugger – his face was covered up. 'Take off your watch!' That was all he said.

When I bought that watch – a Franck Muller Vanguard, worth about £70,000 and studded with diamonds – I couldn't wait to see what it looked like on my wrist. Now

I couldn't get it off quick enough. I looked away from my assailant all the time. I didn't want to see that gun. If he was going to shoot me, I didn't want to see it happening. I also wanted him to see that I wasn't going to retaliate and so kept my hands close to my side as much as I could, not easy as a boxer — every instinct when someone is coming at you is to cover your face, or go on the attack.

The last thing I wanted was to make a sudden movement and make him panic, although the temptation to go back at him was always there. Remember those men who tried to steal my car? They had seen that side of me. I'm only human. If someone on the street says something to me, or starts on me, I switch. I'm a fighter. You punch me and I'll punch you back. Being a professional boxer doesn't change that. It doesn't mean I'll only do it in a ring with a crowd of 20,000 and a coach in the corner. I'll defend myself and that's that. Five, six people — it doesn't matter.

This, though, was no time for heroics. 'Take the watch! There you go, man.' It was scary. I didn't want to make it any worse. I mean, what's the point of fighting back in a situation like that? A watch could be replaced but my life couldn't. It wasn't just me either. There were a lot of people around if he started firing. And he wasn't alone. There were two other men with him, although I had no idea that was the case until afterwards. Did they have weapons too? If it all kicked off, what was their reaction going to be? As it was, they got what they wanted quickly and without any resistance. That was it, they were in a car and off.

The whole thing was a blur. It lasted no more than a few seconds. I said exactly that to the Flying Squad officer who screeched up just minutes later. He told me that most people remember muggings as lasting several minutes. I was the exact opposite, again maybe because I was a boxer, used to seeing a confrontation as hundreds of tiny moments each requiring a decision to be made.

Looking back, the whole thing probably played out as best it could. What if I'd jumped in my car and they'd chased me? Or an innocent passer-by had been hurt? I'm so glad Faryal wasn't stood next to me when he pointed the gun because I know she would have panicked, which would only have made things worse. Later she was worried she might get hate on social media for not being there alongside me, for running off to the other side of the street. I couldn't believe what I was hearing. Are there really people out there who think like that? It's a man with a gun, not Romeo and Juliet. She did exactly the right thing.

I thought back to earlier that day. 'Why do we have to go to east London?' Faryal had said to me. But to me there wasn't an issue. It's a place where I have a big fan base, and there's some great food round there. Yes, I'd heard stories about people getting robbed but that can happen anywhere and, like everybody, I never thought it would happen to me.

Why assume people want to take advantage? It's part of being me to be approached by strangers for selfies, autographs, a quick chat, whatever, and I've always been totally cool with that. I'm not someone who views everything as a negative. I'm a humble guy like that, but Faryal always said I needed to be careful, especially since I have always liked wearing fancy watches. From that point of view, the robbery was a wake-up call. Not everyone out there is a friend.

We weren't due to fly back to Dubai for another few days. I'll be honest, for the rest of the time, whenever I was out and about, I did feel scared. I was paranoid. When something like that happens you suddenly start seeing danger everywhere. Actually, maybe that isn't paranoia – it's common sense. Who wouldn't be wary after having a gun pointed at them? Faryal still looks over her shoulder now.

Up to that point I'd never used bodyguards – I used to think people who did that kind of stuff were a bit full of themselves. I've never fallen back on fame as a reason to be distant. If anything, I wanted it to bring me closer – as in the 'people's champion'. I always wanted to be around people, there for people. If you're going to be distant, no way can you do that.

But after the robbery I did start thinking about protection. There were times when I felt uncomfortable, like one day when me and Faryal were in London and it got dark very quickly. It was only six o'clock but we found ourselves walking down a quiet side street and I couldn't stop thinking about how easy it would be for people to be watching us, to ambush us and rob us. I also thought how sad it was that it had come to that. How I'd gone from 'everything will be fine' to wondering who might be round the next corner.

It's incredible to think the UK now has so much crime, people getting shot, stabbed. I've never been scared to go anywhere in the world, but if anything was to go wrong I never thought it would happen in the UK, especially on a public street at a busy time. It's one of the reasons I've come to love Dubai and spend so much of my time there. I've never felt unsafe in Dubai. I miss the UK a lot but will always put my family's security first, and that's why if we are in the UK now, we will occasionally have security with us. I don't mean like in America where famous people will have four or five massive security guards with them all the time. I'm talking someone who understands where the car should be parked, what entrance and exit to use, what to do if something goes wrong.

Sadly, you never know who's following your movements. Earlier on the day of the robbery I'd done a selfie in Oxford Street. I was wearing the watch then, same as I had the night before at an event at the Grosvenor House Hotel in Mayfair. As always, pictures of me were all over social media. I'd never really thought about it, but it is a bit like having your every position posted online.

If that whole horrible incident taught me anything it's that trouble can strike at any time. I still think about it a lot – what it was like to have someone stick a gun in my face with their finger on the trigger. I wonder what sort of life someone must be living to point a gun at a stranger in the street. What is that person going through to make them do that? Desperate times make for desperate people. Some people might think I'm mad for even thinking about my attackers' lives, but there's a reason behind everything. If I was in their shoes, in their lives, and was having a tough time, who knows how I'd act? I'm not saying I'd be doing what they did, but times are hard for many, many people. When everything is lost, people will take what they can and run. It saddens me – someone who is young and desperate, they don't know what they have to lose. I mean, is stealing a watch worth spending year after year staring at a cell door?

The police didn't waste much time catching the culprits – and they were thankfully convicted in early

2023. Not only were there multiple witnesses but the whole thing was caught on CCTV, which also showed the staff of the Sahara Grill restaurant in Leyton, where we'd just eaten, rushing to my aid, for which I will always be grateful. They were willing to put themselves in a dangerous situation for me. I wish they hadn't but it makes you feel very humble when people act like that. This wasn't pretend. This wasn't a boxing match. There wasn't a referee. Later the owner said they had acted not because of who I was but because of what I was – a dad with three kids. I thought that was incredible. And people say boxers are brave.

. . .

Maybe I wouldn't have been wearing a watch like that if I hadn't been a fighter. I'm not stupid. I realise it's boxing which has created this whole different multi-dimensional life for me. But I was always determined to be the best I could, to have the good things in life and, in business or whatever, I'd have found a way to do it.

People say to me: 'But you're a fighter. Why do you think you could have succeeded in something else?' I tell them to look at how I did what I did – by putting every possible distraction to one side. And when you're young, there are a lot of distractions! While everyone else was partying, I was in a gym sweating blood. When I came back from the Olympics I didn't let it go to my head. And when I turned professional, I challenged myself again, always taking the toughest fights I could. Put that approach into real life instead of sport and there's no reason the results shouldn't be the same.

Just look at my foundation. The fact is, almost ten years from when I first set it up, the charity is still doing incredible work. One of the proudest moments of my life was when the foundation launched a project to build a hospital in Matore – remember, in the Punjab province where my family is from? The announcement was made in the wake of the Covid pandemic which caused so much pain in Pakistan, as it did everywhere else.

The foundation is a source of great motivation for me. I've never wanted to live in a bubble removed from real life, and whenever I see disaster, hunger and poverty around the world I always want to help. Having kids has only made me feel other people's pain more. Looking at children being pulled from the wreckage of the 2023 earthquake in Turkey and Syria, I couldn't help seeing the faces of my own in the same situation, and, through the foundation, several tonnes of aid was soon on its way.

We live in difficult times and I know that sadly there will always be work to be done. I see it in Pakistan. A lot has improved in recent years as regards alleviating poverty and inequality but there remains so much to do and I'll always try to be a voice for those who haven't been as lucky in life as I have. Someone recently asked me if I might one day try to enter politics in Pakistan. It's not a closed door, and I met the now ousted Prime Minister and cricketing hero Imran Khan a few times, but for now I'm happy for my foundation to do the work through emergency relief and long-term projects. I am also determined to promote boxing in the country. Already I have an Amir Khan Academy in Islamabad, and I'm hopeful of providing more facilities elsewhere.

I know my academies work from the examples of those in Bolton and Peterborough in the UK. Yes, they're places where people can learn to box, but they're also about keeping kids off the street and educating them on issues such as knife crime. In the fifteen years since I set up my gym in Bolton around 200,000 kids have been through its doors. If just one of those has been diverted from the wrong side of the tracks then every minute of those fifteen years will have been worth it. My academies are all about providing safe spaces where people can work out their future paths in a positive way.

Ultimately, God is the one who will decide what path I take, but I do know one thing – I'll always be hands-on in anything I do. People ask why I don't farm everything out to assistants, publicists, PAs. But that's the whole point. I want to be in the thick of it. Anyway, behave like a prima donna in Bolton and I'd soon get pulled down a peg or two! I think it's that whole attitude of 'don't get ideas above yourself' that initially stopped me exhibiting my boxing memorabilia in the house.

Some people wonder why this old Lancashire town remains such a big part of my life – 'But, mate, everyone knows who you are here. You could go anywhere and not be bothered.' Well, for one, I never see anyone coming up and saying hello as 'being bothered'. And, for two, it's precisely because everyone knows me that makes living round here so great. In Bolton, they see me all the time. I can go for a run, walk round the town centre, have a pasty with Gary Neville, and people don't bat an eyelid. They give me a smile or say hello like they would anyone else. I could easily have moved a few miles down the road to Manchester but everything that made me who I am is here, and everything I've built for the future is here as well. I want to give back to Bolton what Bolton has given to me.

It's helped me that in normal everyday life I've never had a big ego. As a boxer I did, but that's different – it's a tough sport and to back yourself, big yourself up, is necessary. Otherwise, I've always been myself. Whenever I get asked to a wedding, a birthday party, any event in Bolton, I'll never hide away. I'll go there happily and chat with anyone. It's my home town and I feel comfortable, especially nowadays after the gun incident in London. To some extent I'll always be a target, whether it's people jealous of my success, or potentially something more serious, but in Bolton, like Dubai, I feel very, very safe.

There's another thing about Bolton. It's from here that my true legacy was built. My time in the ring might be done, but as an inspiration I hope my name will be everlasting. People used to say: 'We're Muslim, we're Asian, we can't make it in boxing.' Now that can never be true.

On the undercard at the Kell Brook fight, for instance, was Adam Azim, a young pro with the world at his feet. He came to watch me box when he was six and has spoken of me now 'passing the torch' to his generation. I couldn't be happier to do that. I love the fact that my dad dragging me to Mick Jelley's gym nearly thirty (wow!) years ago is still having an effect today.

Back then I was the only Asian face down there. Now I'll guarantee that pretty much every gym has boxers like me. There are Asian trainers, Asian promoters, Asian coaches. The entire culture around Asians and boxing has changed. Before, many parents would insist their children concentrate solely on their education. Then I came along and showed that the same quality of life – nice house, nice car, nice family, financially secure – can be had by being a talented boxer. Don't get me wrong, I'm not expecting boxing to be mentioned as a career option at school! But it can at least be seen as a sport that has a positive effect on life and growing up in general.

England Boxing – the governing body of amateur boxing clubs in the country – has only recently started to compile data on its members' ethnicity, but the figures have shown an upward trend. In 2022, out of 19,216 registered boxers, 3,294 came from ethnically diverse communities. Five years before, that figure was 1,626. I'm pretty sure that when I started out it barely registered at all.

The message is simple and clear – everyone is welcome. There is no more effective way to get people to understand each other than by mixing together, working to get better at something they enjoy. I have shown that boxing gyms are places that can enrich Asian lives. From that silver medal in Athens, Asian boxing forged a golden future, and that's why it's the moment in my sporting life which I look back on with most fondness. Nothing else makes me feel so great inside.

I wonder if I might one day face the quandary of whether I should give my blessing for my own children to fight. I don't know how I'd feel about that. Another reason to retire was to do so before the kids were old enough to fully understand what boxing is about. I hate the thought of my children getting hurt but at the same time you have to let people find their own way in life. It's said that children are genetically better than their parents. Chris Eubank Jr is a case in point. Already, aged just two, I can see that Zaviyar is really strong, heavy, dense. I've always said I'd never let my children box – it's brutal – but maybe it was meant to be!

Where the next chapters of my life will take me, and what those chapters will contain, who knows? I have a habit of throwing up a few crazy adventures, a few mad controversies, and more than a few plunges into the unknown. I know also that, down the years, I put far too much pressure on myself as a boxer, and mentally I want what follows to be a smoother ride. Finally, I'm happy just to be myself. In boxing, you are seen only in terms of performance. You are a 'boxer'. You are a 'fighter'.

I'm still a fighter, but now I'm Amir Khan.

COACHING SESSION 12

Twelve rounds gone and I'm still standing. My challenge now is out of the ring.

Like most sportspeople, retirement came to me at a younger age than it would most people. But I genuinely do believe it's never too late to try something new.

My next landmark birthday is the big four-zero. I quite like the settled life now, back and forth between Dubai and Bolton. But who knows what's round the corner? And if something special comes my way, do I just say no? As you get older it's harder to take big decisions. But the way I look at it, variety keeps you young. If something appeals, I will always jump at it. And you should too.

That's the lasting lesson I want people to take away from this book – you don't have to sit back and let life happen around you. There is another way. You can jump in feet first. No one can ever predict where you'll end up but there's a pretty good chance you'll enjoy the ride.

That's what I'll keep on doing and I hope you'll carry on doing the same. One thing though – if you end up flat on your back with the referee counting to ten, don't blame me.

ACKNOWLEDGEMENTS

A big thank you to everyone who has helped make this book possible. To wordsmith John Woodhouse, thank you for helping to craft my story. To my publisher Century at Penguin Random House, thank you, team, for all of your support: Ben Brusey, Rachel Kennedy, Cameron Watson, Jason Smith, Jessica Fletcher, Anna Cowling and Joanna Taylor. Heartfelt thanks goes to my brilliant literary agent Natalie Jerome, to Gordon Wise at Curtis Brown, to my publicist Nicki Clarke and Nick Hartwell. I want to thank all of my family and friends, and everyone who has been on this wild journey with me. But my biggest thanks must go to my beloved Faryal, Lamaisah, Alayna and Zaviyar. Thank you for making everything possible.

PHOTOGRAPH CREDITS

Inset 1

Page 1, Top photograph © Alex Livesey/Stringer via Getty Images
Bottom photograph © Nigel Roddis/Stringer via Getty Images

Page 2, Top left photograph © Doug Pesinger/Staff via Getty Images
Top right photograph © Al Bello/ Staff via Getty Images

Page 4, Top photograph © Alex Livesey/Staff via Getty Images
Bottom photograph © JOHN GURZINSKI/ Stringer via Getty Images

Page 5, Top photograph © Ethan Miller/Staff via Getty Images
Bottom photograph © Ed Mulholland/Golden Boy/Contributor via Getty Images

Page 6, All photographs © Al Bello/Staff via Getty Images

Inset 2

Page 1, Bottom right photograph © ITV/Shutterstock
Page 3, Top left photograph © John Gichigi/Staff via Getty Images

INDEX

INDEX